Enjoy the memories!

Hope Irvin Marston

Isaiah 40:31

PATRICIA LORENZ

GREAT AMERICAN OUTHOUSE STORIES

The Hole Truth And Nothing Butt

Copyright © 2004 by Patricia Lorenz

ISBN 0-7414-1882-7

Published by:

PUBLISHING.COM

519 West Lancaster Avenue
Haverford, PA 19041-1413
Info@buybooksontheweb.com
www.buybooksontheweb.com
Toll-free (877) BUY BOOK
Local Phone (610) 520-2500
Fax (610) 519-0261

Printed in the United States of America

Printed on Recycled Paper

Published January 2004

Dedicated to:

My four children, their spouses, my grand-children; Grandpa William Porter Knapp whose own outhouse provided my first opportunity to discover the fun and lore of America's outhouses; and my dad, Edward J. Kobbeman, who built and raced a few outhouses and taught me about love, laughter and living life to the fullest.

Infinity Publishing
Haverford, PA

CONTENTS

INTRODUCTION

As one of the first baby boomers born right after World War II ended in 1945, I was fortunate to grow up in a brand new modern ranch-style home in Rock Falls, Illinois, the house my Dad, a former WWII fighter pilot, built in 1947. That house has modern everything: electric kitchen, laundry room, a radiant heating system with hot water pipes in the floors so all the floors are toasty warm, and an especially-nice, full service bathroom.

However, my sense of *modern* flew the coop every time we visited Grandpa and Grandma Knapp, my mother's folks in Blandinsville, Illinois, a tiny town three hours to the south. Even though they lived in town with close neighbors and sidewalks, Grandpa saw no need for an indoor bathroom. No sir, that outhouse out back did just fine. Easy for him to say.

That outhouse was such an amazement to my young mind that each time I saw or was forced to use an outhouse during my growing-up years and beyond, I became more and more interested in the lore, history, inspiration and humor that outhouses seem to evoke everywhere in America.

In 1994 when I attended the Mark Twain Writer's Conference in Hannibal, Illinois, I announced to the gathering that I was collecting true outhouse stories and would put the best ones in a book. I collected stories for the next ten years from people ages 13-94 from all over the country, from New York to California, Texas to Michigan, from seventeen states altogether. Many of the authors in this book are people I've never met, but who certainly do write a fine yarn about their own outhouse memories. I thank them all, young and old, far and near, for their contributions.

These stories combine the rich history that the American outhouse has woven among generations of families with the wit, wisdom and inspiration of those who used the outdoor privies in days gone by and in places, may still be using them today.

Patricia Lorenz

THANK YOU TO:

The great Americans from sea to shining sea who wrote these outhouse stories and shared their special, heartfelt memories in this book.

Melanie Rigney, whose friendship, encouragement, and editing of this book made the whole process so much easier and lots more fun.

James Auer, the Milwaukee Journal/Sentinel art critic, who blurted out the subtitle, *The Hole Truth and Nothing Butt* at our *Allied Authors* meeting one night.

My cousin Jean and her husband George Ransom who helped me find and photograph the splendid outhouse on the cover and my dad, Ed Kobbeman, for posing in front of it.

The entire staff at Infinity Publishing, who, without exception, helped make the birthing of this book a joy-filled experience from beginning to end...and that's the truth, the hole truth and nothing butt.

THE OUTHOUSE

By Janet Armato

As I recall,
it was about the size
of a confessional.
Within it
I would realize
(aware of both my
purpose and intent)
the meaning of my life
and how it had been spent.
In the silence
of a woods or rural yard,
I could contemplate
how lax or hard
my efforts to redeem
myself from sin had been.
So, too, could I review
the blessings I received,
the losses that I grieved,
and dream the dreams
I yet hoped to achieve.
Though it was often dark,
there was a crescent crevice
through which ambient light
could glow, would glow,
letting me know that
no matter how difficult life seemed,
no matter what my plight,
every burden passes
and, in the end, even
the most trying times
come out all right.

WHEN THE JETSONS VISITED THE FLINTSTONES

By Patricia Lorenz

It wasn't that long ago actually, back in the early 1950s. Recent enough that nearly everyone in America had indoor plumbing and either oil, gas or electric heat.

But not my Grandfather. Living in the tiny, eye-blink town of Blandinsville in central Illinois, William Porter Knapp was caught in a half-century time warp that hung around his 100-year-old white frame house like a veiled stranger from another century.

Grandpa's house and the buildings surrounding it were out of touch with modern times - so much so that when I was a little girl and we'd leave our modern brick home with electric everything and drive three hours to Grandpa's house, I always felt we were taking an adventure into yesteryear. It was like the Jetsons going to visit the Flintstones. As soon as we pulled up in front of Grandpa's house I knew right away I wasn't residing in the electric age any longer.

The old, squeaky porch swing was the first clue. Grandpa would be waiting for us in the swing, moving only an inch or two in each direction, concentrating intently on something or other. I never did figure out what it was he thought about so hard in that swing, but I did experience how relaxing the old thing was. To this day I long for a porch swing - if I just had a front porch, that is.

After a quick "Hello, Grandpa!" hug, I'd open the wobbly, wooden-framed front screen, step inside and come face to face with the second dead giveaway that this house was not a member of modern times.

The big, old, black coal stove was a contraption plopped smack-dab in the middle of the living room. Grandpa tended

2

that stove (the only heat source for the house) with the love and dedication of a microbiologist tending his cultures.

Every morning at sunup Grandpa could be heard shaking the grate to loosen up the leftover embers, dropping sooty coal into the innards of that old stove, and then lighting it with long wooden kitchen matches and newspapers so it could belch and clank and keep us warm all day and all night.

But the one thing that really set Grandpa's house apart from all the other homes in the little neighborhood was the outhouse out back. The outhouse was mysterious. Downright foreboding, if you want to know the truth - at least to my six-year-old mind.

I remember clutching Momma's hand late at night, shuffling along the sidewalk in my fluffy bedroom slippers as we made our last trip of the day to Grandpa's old time-and-weather worn outhouse.

It wasn't a trip I looked forward to. Even though Grandpa's home was filled with comfortable, overstuffed furniture in the living room, comforter-lined rockers in the front of the coal stove and fluffy mattresses topped with feather pillows in each bedroom, Grandpa obviously didn't give a hoot about the comforts of life when it came to the *necessary* house out back.

The outside of this windowless building was parched gray clapboard. Once the visitor was safe inside, the squeaky door slammed shut with the help of a tight spring at the top of the door. The inside was, well, smelly - and not just a little bit smelly, either.

This was a two-seater outhouse, superior to a one-seater, I suppose, although at first I couldn't figure out why. Availing oneself of its use didn't seem to be something one did in pairs...until, that is, my first trip to the outhouse at night. Clutching my mother's hand and insisting that she join me for every outhouse adventure after dark became a ritual. I could even understand why some outhouses had three or four seats. Mama and all the little kids in the "Little House on the Prairie"

3

days could no doubt cut down on their outhouse time considerably if they all went together.

Of course there was no light in Grandpa's outhouse so each nighttime adventure out there, in the cool weather especially, was one that I tried to make as brief as possible. A quick hop off the well-worn, old gray plank seat and off I'd run, letting the springed door slam behind me - not caring at that point whether or not Mother was still perched on her half of the facilities.

I'd run back down that sidewalk, past the garden, under the mammoth grape arbor, past the wooden tables covered with ripening apples and tomatoes, past the water pump and back into the mud porch, just off Grandpa's kitchen.

I'd slip across the shiny linoleum floor of the kitchen - a room warmed only by the wood cooking stove if somebody happened to be cooking something--on into the dining room and right over to the tall oak buffet where Grandpa kept a Depression glass jar filled with sugary lemon drops.

I'd pop one of those yellow beauties into my mouth and then plop down on one of the rocking chairs in the living room to watch a little television with Grandpa before bedtime.

It always amazed me that my grandfather was one of the first people in his town to get a television set in the 1950s but was one of the last ones to install indoor plumbing. There must have been something simple, something comforting about that old outhouse for Grandpa, although for the life of me I have yet to discover what it was.

To this day, whenever I'm in the country and happen to see an outhouse that's been preserved as a memory from the past, I think about Grandpa Knapp's home in Blandinsville, and a flood of memories comes back to warm my heart and soul.

Well, most of them warm my heart, anyway. The ones about my trips to the outhouse late at night in the cold air - well, I like to save those memories, spice 'em up a bit, and use 'em for ghost stories to tell my kids.

Forgive me, Grandpa.

ODE TO A COMMODE

By Wally Winston

It stood proud and pretty on the immaculate lawn in the front yard of our modern ranch home in the elite suburb of Greendale, one of Milwaukee's finest and yuppiest of villages.

"Winston, what in heaven's name are you doing now?" asked a neighbor as he scratched his head in amazement.

"Wife wanted another bathroom, but couldn't afford the plumbing," was my twinkle-in-the-eye reply.

When my wife, Shirley, gave our son and me notice that she wasn't going with us to our hunting shack up north until we built an outhouse, we thought about Shirley's wonderful cooking during our weekend hunting trips. Then we immediately began to wonder how we could build an outhouse without interfering with our grouse, woodcock and pheasant hunting. We also had to have mornings and evenings available to bow hunt the elusive whitetail deer in the area. But I understood Shirley's concern. None of us enjoyed doing our business in the primitive honey bucket at the foot of the bunk beds in the hunting shack.

The solution came in a blinding flash, typical of die-hard hunters. Why not build the outhouse on the front lawn of our "real" home back in the Milwaukee suburb, where tools and electricity were right inside the garage? We could build it after supper on weekdays, then trailer it northward to the hunting shack, thus saving the weekends for the great hunt.

Work on the comfort johnny went well and what emerged a few weeks later was indeed a splendid specimen of an outhouse. The sloped roof gave it a graceful look. Shirley happened to be at the city dump one day -- not one of her usual hangouts, mind you -- where she found a perfectly good French door with fifteen small window panes on the top half. Naturally, she hauled it home for the privy. When

5

she realized that those fifteen windows detracted somewhat from one's privacy factor, she quickly located equally superb venetian blinds at the local Goodwill store. After painting our pristine privy a reddish brown simulated redwood color, the outhouse was complete, except, of course, for the interior details.

I added a hook on the inside wall to hang one's coat or bathrobe and then built a shelf for magazines. Next, I nailed the bottom side of a two-pound coffee can to the wall to hold the toilet paper and foil-wrapped wet towelettes. The plastic lid on the end of the can kept the mice out of the toilet paper. A bucket of lime in the corner helped eliminate odors. And finally, the crowning glory of my privy accessories was "ye olde cozy." I found a square gray corduroy lawn chair cushion somewhere and cut a big circle out of the center of it...large enough for the most ample bottom. Then I stitched around the edges of the exposed foam rubber to give it a finished look. The cozy hung on a hook on the inside wall just to the left of the seat, and believe me, on many a frosty morning my backside was mighty glad to land on the cozy instead of the ice-crystaled bare wood.

During those weeks of outhouse production in suburban Milwaukee, many a neighbor admiringly asked just how long my work of art was going to remain standing on our front lawn. We even had a visit from the village building inspector one day, a gentleman I recognized as I peeked around the picture window curtain and then quickly decided I wasn't home when he rang the bell.

We also had a neighbor ask to rent the outhouse for his annual family reunion picnic but I declined because of legal problems it could cause. (Over the years I have abided by the law on numerous occasions.)

Some of the neighbors, however, actually wanted that outhouse out of there, if you can believe it. When several of the more humorous types hinted that they might begin to use it, I decided it was time to move it to its final destination...hunter's paradise in the north woods.

6

We were delighted when our neighbors practically jumped at the chance to help us load the thing onto the matching utility trailer for its journey to Jackson County. The man across the street even launched our portable potty with a bottle of beer and wished us bon voyage.

You can imagine my sense of accomplishment and pride as our four-hour northbound journey on Wisconsin's busy interstate highways caused quite a few heads to turn as our perky little privy stood upright in the small trailer. I felt as if I was transporting a monument of sorts that proclaimed for all the world my sense of creativity and woodworking genius.

I'm also quite sure that when this magnificent structure was put into place in the woods near our tarpaper hunting shack, our property value skyrocketed. That outhouse is still standing, some forty years later, proudly performing its most basic of human functions.

Since our hunting shack didn't have running water, we decided a few seasons later to add an outdoor shower right behind the outhouse, thus making our grand privy a one-and-a-half bath facility. A simple rubber mat on the ground to stand on and a five-gallon container painted black, then hoisted onto the outhouse roof, completed the addition. It worked great, providing the sun was shining to warm the water in the black bucket above.

Over the years I've done a lot of thinking, meditation and problem solving inside that outhouse. However, the most memorable moment occurred one early morning in November a few months after we added the shower stall.

While sleeping in one of the bunks in the hunting shack Mother Nature sent a gripping message to my alimentary canal, forcing me to raise my consciousness out of many levels of deep slumber, caused mostly by the previous night's successful hunt and the celebration thereafter.

I lumbered out of my sleeping bag in my altogether and headed for the simulated redwood commode in the woods with my faithful hunting dog, Blaze, who joined me for a similar reason. The rising sun, shining right into the outhouse door, was warm and welcoming, causing me to leave the door wide open. We were, after all, a mile from the nearest neighbor.

My hunting companion solved her needs and wandered around to check things out. In the meantime, I began to slip back a couple of levels into comforting sleep. That warm morning sun felt good on my bare buck legs as I sat on the smooth redwood seat underneath the cozy that circled my buck naked fanny.

Suddenly Blaze began to chase a red squirrel back and forth in front of the outhouse. When the frightened creature couldn't reach a tree in time to make his escape, he dove down the drainage hole formed by the continual flow of shower water in the back of the country commode.

At this point I have to try to understand the dilemma of the poor, hysterical red squirrel and only guess at his frustration. Envision him racing along that drainage hole that flowed directly into the terrible smelly black pit directly under the seat of the outhouse. Once he slipped into the terrible pit, the only light and hope of escape for Mr. Squirrel was to jump up toward the shaft of light emanating between the front of my body and the toilet seat. Escape was only a few feet away if he could just hurl himself toward the light.

Well, he hurled himself, all right, but he missed the edge of the seat by inches. In order to keep from falling back down into what was certainly no bed of roses he clung to parts of my manhood I'd rather not remember, thank you. Suffice it to say, my sleep level indicator shot into the red zone like a rocket. One minute I was dozing in the warm sunlight letting it all hang out and the next moment a furry creature had his claws firmly embedded in and was passionately clinging to the family jewels.

I let out a bass bellow that vibrated and trembled into a soprano shriek that not only woke my wife in our shack across the woods, but also woke the neighbor in his shack a mile down the road. As I shot off the seat like a missile I probably knocked that squirrel senseless as his body hit the front edge of the commode and he slipped back into the dark hole below.

I continued to scream and jump up and down in my altogether...only calming down when I finally figured out what had happened.

The morning wasn't a total waste since my blessed wife volunteered to apply medication to my wounds. Trouble is, as I knelt on the bed on all fours, squirming in obvious pain and discomfort, she alternated between her Florence Nightingale duties and falling off her chair in uncontrollable fits of laughter.

Sometimes I don't understand my wife one bit; however, I do have to give her credit for her unusual *point of view* if you get my drift.

All I can say is that most times *getting close to nature* is a pleasant experience for a hunter like me, but I think that particular early morning constitutional adventure in the old outhouse is one outdoor experience I could have done without quite well. But in spite of that single event, the old outhouse and I have shared many special moments over the years and will continue to do so as long as there's hunting to be done and land on which to do it.

TWENTY GIRLS AND AN OUTHOUSE

By Guinevere Robin Petrousky

Winter camping. I don't know where my troop leader got that idea, but it wasn't one of her better ones.

"Outhouses? In January? Are you out of your mind?" was the nicest thing anyone said. At least we were staying in a nice warm lodge, right?

The entire trip up to Camp Trefoil was spent in a fascinating debate on what would happen to skin touching a toilet seat at thirty below zero.

"Please tell me you're kidding!" I begged. "I need indoor toilets!"

My troop leader just murmured, "Girl Scout camping builds character."

We reached the lodge intact and did all the things girls do...jumping on tables when someone mentioned mice, screaming, running around, acting normal.

Night falls quickly in the woods and that night our need to use the bathroom facilities and nightfall happened at the same time. The outhouse was not near the lodge. After walking out of the lodge and clambering over the porch, we hugged the center of the trail and stuck close together as our flashlights bounced off each other and the woods. We walked and sang down the hill crossed the road, entered into the woods again, and after what seemed like a couple of miles... there it was. There is no smell quite like that smell. In fact, it is that particular odor that makes it easy to find an outhouse on a dark summer night.

This particular outhouse had two stalls, each with its own door.

"Guin, go ahead." Jessica urged me on.

"No! You go!" I said.

"Hey, we'll get Kellie to go!" Jessica whispered.

"Go on, Kellie," I whispered, giving her shoulder a shove.

Kellie frowned at both of us, "I AM going! I can't wait any longer."

Jessica went into the other stall. When Kellie was finished, I stepped in but not before I was assured that no lurking toilet monsters resided within.

As soon as Jessica opened the door on her stall to come out she screamed, "Eiiiahhhhhhh!" Scared to death, I burst out of the other stall.

"What happened?" I gasped. Jessica was hightailing it down the trail. I ran after her, heart pounding.

"Don't leave me!" Kellie screamed, "Help!"

At last we caught up to Jessica. "What did you see? What was it?"

Jessica looked sheepish as she caught her breath. "I think it was a squirrel."

Within a few days we twenty Girl Scouts were old hands at the whole business, thanks to a storm and a downed power line that left us stranded at camp "good times" for a few extra days.

Each day, coming up from the outhouse, we'd make friends with girls we didn't know so well. The great icebreaker was, "It sure stinks in there, doesn't it?"

"Sure does," the girl would answer and then we'd chat all the way back to the lodge. By nightfall we'd all be around the campfire recalling our most awful outhouse adventures.

I still hate outhouses. Even though they do make for better social circles.

PASTOR IN THE OUTHOUSE

By Rev. James C. Hefley

Years ago, my friend Reverend Tal Bonham served as pastor of a small-town Baptist church in Texas when he was a student at Southwestern Baptist Theological Seminary.

Tal was a sensitive young man who had difficulty relating to people. He served the church on weekends, spending Friday and Saturday nights in the parsonage and returning to seminary on Monday.

The church was built on a hill. Beside it perched an ancient unisex outhouse. The parsonage was built beside the post office at the foot of the hill. The parsonage did not have an outhouse, nor did it have indoor plumbing.

Saturday mornings, the town loafers, sitting on a bench in front of the post office, watched the young minister climb the hill to the outhouse. Tal could hear them chuckling and feel their stares on his back as he started up the hill. He felt his face turn crimson, presuming they were talking about him. The next morning he saw them in church and felt embarrassed when speaking to them. The church, by Tal's recollection, was dead and cold and he did not feel any great love for the people.

One memorable Saturday Tal ascended to the outhouse, feeling the stares of the loafers. He shuffled into the little building and closed the door. Suddenly, a sharp gust of wind blew the outhouse over, exposing Tal to all viewers as he tumbled down the hill. The loafers collapsed in uproarious laughter as Tal rolled to a stop.

Red-faced, Tal quickly pulled up his pants and was preparing to run for his dignity when suddenly he grasped the absurdity of his situation. The young preacher began laughing. The more he laughed, the more the loafers howled. All of them, including Tal, were still laughing the next morning in church.

Years later, when recalling the incident, Tal told me, "When the wind blew the outhouse over, I learned to laugh at myself. That broke the ice in that cold church and a revival resulted."

Tal advanced in the ministry to become executive director of the Ohio Baptist Convention. He died in the early 1990s after many long years of faithful service.

BANTY ROOSTER RULED THE OUTHOUSE

By Irene Haring

I was born in 1909, and I remember when I was a child living on a farm we had a nice outhouse. We also had a nice catalog inside that outhouse for necessary reasons. On the outside was a not-so-nice banty rooster. Whenever I'd visit the outhouse, that pesky banty rooster waited and watched right by the door. As soon as you would come out, it would dive at your legs and peck the life out of you! As a small child it was very scary for me, even if he was a little fellow. His beak felt like a red-hot pick. So there I'd sit, inside the outhouse, much longer than necessary, reading and rereading the catalog. I'd sit and read, hoping that rooster would leave, but he never did. I'll never forget that little devil with the mighty peck.

MACHIGUENGA OUTHOUSES

By Ron Snell

Born and raised in the Amazon rain forest in Peru where my parents were missionaries, I learned to walk, talk and play with the Machiguenga Indians. My parents, brother, sisters and I lived in a land where outhouses were a way of life. However, the outhouses in Machiguenga land were pretty wild. The Indians had traditionally used the river or the forest for their stands and squats, but sooner or later it was inevitable that they would be taught to store their poop in the ground instead of letting it float off down river, feeding the fish along the way. (We used to catch some really big fish just down from the villages.)

Anyway, having the idea of an outhouse isn't the same as having an outhouse, so there were usually a few parts missing. For starters, the Machis were used to squatting instead of sitting. After all, who in their right mind would put their bottom right where someone else just had? So they just dug a big hole, put a platform of crisscrossed palm planks over it and left a hole to squat over.

Mind you, that squatting hole was only there to satisfy sanitation experts – it had nothing to do with actually using the outhouse. It was so tiny about the only way you could hit it was with a funnel, the advantage being that although it would be nearly impossible to get your serious business into it, it was equally difficult for you to fall through it and for wild animals to climb out of it while you were feeling particularly vulnerable in the middle of dark nights.

Even though you couldn't get poop into it to save your soul, it was terribly easy to get your flashlight into it, and there is the story of the flashlight that fell in, stuck in the muck and illuminated our backsides until the local equivalent of the Energizer bunny died.

Presumably the essence of the outhouse is the hole...not the house. Or perhaps an outhouse without a house is just an *out*. We had one of those in the village of Monte Carmelo, and considered it a night-time-only *out*. Even then it had its risks. One night my dad was happily squatting to get an all-day load off his mind when he heard a snort. Dad whipped around with his flashlight and nearly hit the village bull full in the face. Dad said he was almost finished with his job before the bull visited, but that bull got a bit more out of him!

Some of the outhouses had walls, but the walls were made from split palm or cane, so they weren't terribly private. In fact, if you had any sense of modesty at all, you kept using the forest or the river. Mom was squatting one afternoon and heard a sniffle. She turned to see a little boy staring at her through the cracks, which was good because the boy had run away from home and now he was found. So was Mom, though she wasn't particularly happy about it.

And if those outhouses had walls, they often didn't have doors, which meant that the cows could come right in and savor the Charmin to their hearts' content. One cow even got a lunch of three months' worth of Mom's sanitary supplies, with the nearest replacements in a store about 350 miles away as the crow (or little Cessna) flies. That had to make for an interesting cud.

But I suppose the most interesting Machiguenga outhouse was the one they made for a special celebration in the village of Huallana. After 30 years of hard work, my folks had finished translating the New Testament into Machiguenga and the village leaders wanted to have a grand celebration to dedicate the recently arrived Scriptures. Guests would include Machiguengas from other villages as well as key supporters and members from my parents' home church.

Since the Machis are terribly hospitable and want to meet a guest's every bio-need, they pondered long and hard about the outhouse situation. A few had been to the outside world and knew that where the white man came from, there were outhouses for men and ones for women, each with an appropriate sign to make sure no one got confused. So that was what they would do--make the first pair of sex-distinguished outhouses in Machiguenga history.

Materials, of course, weren't easy to come by. They'd have to gather leaves from the jungle for the thatched roof; collect palm trunks to split for the walls and floor; and cut vines to lash the whole thing together. The point is, that although they wanted to make it right, they couldn't afford to make it extravagant. It would be only about four feet tall, which was fine for a squatting Machiguenga who had to just pull her robe up. But not so fine for a gringa who had to half undress to squat.

The end result sat proudly just on the other side of the airstrip from the church where the dedication would be held. It boasted a new roof and walls with the rich smell of the forest. Two deep holes had been dug underneath to accommodate whatever load might be dropped. A sign on the left said *Women* and a sign on the right said *Men.*

And...hmmm...no wall between the two holes.

FIVE LITTLE OUTHOUSE STORIES

By Rita L. Stobbe

THE LAP OF LUXURY

A store owner went to use the outhouse late in the evening one summer, leaving the door unlatched because of the lateness of the hour. Unaware that he had left the house, his wife headed for the outhouse as well. She opened the door, and following appropriate preparations she sat down – landing on her husband's lap. She screamed bloody murder and without turning around, headed for the house in double quick time. The amused husband sat and laughed at his wife's discomfiture. Because they lived in town the outhouse was accessible to others, so it wasn't until the next day that she discovered whose lap she had sat on – when her husband regaled one of his customers with his previous night's experience.

MYSTERY CARGO

Late one Halloween night in an all-night coffee shop in southern Alberta, Canada, a police officer and several local citizens were swapping stories about Halloween escapades.

"When I was a teen," the police officer said, "several of us got into a truck and gathered up outhouses from farms and hauled them to the railway. We loaded them into a boxcar and sealed it. I've often wondered what happened to them."

One of the locals, a retired Canadian Pacific Railway switchman, exclaimed, "So that's how they got into the car!" He immediately had everyone's attention. "I was in New Brunswick, clear across Canada, when a yard maintenance man called me aside and showed me a boxcar sitting on a siding. He said no one knew what to do with it, since there was no paperwork with it. We decided it was time to find out what was in it, so we broke the lock and opened up the car. It was filled with outhouses! And to think they came from this area."

BATHROOM MAGIC

My parents lived in a rural community where outhouses still dotted the landscape. We had come from Chicago to join them for Christmas. Our children, who knew nothing but inside plumbing, were about to be introduced to what I had grown up with.

After their first visit to one of these ancient outdoor relics they both came dashing into the house, eyes wide with wonder over their great discovery.

"Mom, Grandma's bathroom is magic! You don't have to flush!" they reported breathlessly.

A QUICK EXIT

As a young bride my aunt was visiting her in-laws for the first time. Needing to visit the restroom, she was pointed to the outside "biffy." She was about to sit down when she heard a warning rattle. Looking down at the floor she saw a large rattlesnake. How did she escape? Very quickly!

A TWO-STORY WONDER

Heritage Park in Calgary, Canada, features one of the most unusual tourist attractions I have ever seen. In its pioneer village is the old Cochran Hotel and behind it is a two-story outhouse. The upper level was for hotel guests, while the lower level was for beer parlor patrons. I guess after you've imbibed freely you don't much care what goes on overhead.

THREE LITTLE OUTHOUSE STORIES

By Les Stobbe

TEEN DREAMS

For an adolescent boy in western Canada, the outhouse was a refuge. Not only could you not be summoned into the field to clear the land of stumps and brush, you could savor the models in bras in the T. Eaton Company mail order catalog – at a time when you were not even permitted to see your sisters in swimwear, much less undies. You could also dream of wearing new clothing you would never see, since your family was still shopping the Goodwill store for everything except denim pants. There were times in January and early February, however, when that refuge was too cold, since temperatures could drop to way below zero and even the wooden seat could chill your bottom.

HALLOWEEN PRANKS

During my growing up years, the outhouse was a primary object of Halloween pranksters in our part of western Canada. Not only were they tipped, loaded on trucks and left at a corner in full view a mile or more away, they were, upon occasion, hoisted onto an absent homeowner's roof. On our farm, all lights stayed on late into the night on Halloween while we made regular visits to the outhouse as a deterrent to such pranksters.

A FAREWELL TO THRONES

One of my favorite stories about outhouses hit the Canadian papers January 1st, 1967, the start of Canada's centennial. It seems that in a town in Manitoba, folks were privy to a unique event the night before. On December 31st, 1966, to celebrate the completion of their $350,000 water and sewage system, the community set fire to 26 outhouses shortly after they'd been paraded through town. Happy citizens, who now had indoor plumbing, cheered the mighty throne fire that was still glowing at dawn's early light as they welcomed the beginning of Canada's 100th year.

BOOTLEGGER'S OUTHOUSE

By Velma Adams

During Prohibition in the late 1920s, our neighbor Ray, his wife and two small children lived in the farmhouse on his father's farm, south of the small town of Tampico in northern Illinois. Ray helped his father part time with farming, but he was well known around the area as a bootlegger, selling alcohol secretly. The county sheriff stopped by many times and checked the house and farm buildings trying to find Ray's stock of liquor, but never found anything.

In the 1930s, my husband's father bought the farm from Ray's dad and in 1947, my husband and I purchased it. We had milk cows so my husband, Eldon, remodeled the barn with stanchions and feed bunks.

One day, Eldon ran into Ray on the street in town and remarked that during the barn renovations he expected to find Ray's hiding place for his bootleg liquor. Ray laughed and said, "You won't find it in the barn. I hid it all in the outhouse! That outhouse had a sturdy concrete foundation with sliding floor boards at one end. There was a wide shelf under the floor, big enough to keep four five-gallon jugs of the best doggone hooch in this country."

Sad to say, some 40 years ago, our high school-age sons hauled that old outhouse to Tampico for the high school homecoming bonfire. That night, unbeknownst to us, a little bit of history went up in flames.

The old outhouse's solid concrete foundation still stands on our farm with colorful flowers growing in it...a fitting tribute to our colorful old friend Ray.

THE OUTHOUSE PLAYHOUSE

By Kay Babb Gannon

It wasn't hard to find our outhouse because in the summer the grass was worn down to look like mown hay. During the wet or snowy seasons, boards lay in a crooked line from the house to the outhouse and coal house. We walked on these boards while mud and slush oozed around the board from the weight of our feet.

The outhouse was a fearful place at night. I remember waking up in the middle of the night and nudging my sleeping older sister, Donna. "Donna, I gotta go! Come with me."

"Go back to sleep," she'd mutter. "You'll soon forget it." Her voice trailed off, soft and sleepy.

I'd lie there, desperately trying to forget that the outhouse was by the alley and we were four houses from the railroad tracks. Hobos and bums often came to our house for food. The older kids told us about bums who killed kids with an ax. Finally, I'd fall asleep only to be wakened with a nudge in the ribs.

"Kay, I'm scared and I gotta go. Come with me." How I longed to tell her, "Go and get murdered by the bums or just go to sleep and you'll forget it."

Instead, we'd throw back the covers and race like lightning until we reached the safety of the outhouse. Upon arrival, we looked inside both wooden holes to be sure there were no snakes in there before doing our business and racing back to bed.

By night the outhouse was frightening, but during the day it was part of our playhouse. Our outhouse and the coal house formed a figure 'L' with the outhouse being the lower part of the 'L'. We connected the two doors that opened toward each other. Donna was 17 months older than me.

Thus, by seniority, she got the coal house for her babies, leaving me with the outhouse.

We papered the walls of the outhouse with old wallpaper and funny papers held up with paste made from water and flour. A long board and old blankets turned the two-holer into our play area. In the coal house, we put newspaper and rugs over carefully stacked coal to form couches and chairs.

Thus, in those World War II days, we pretended that the Nazis were coming to kill our dolls and we had to keep them safe. In our imaginations Donna and I could hear the goose steps of the soldiers searching for our children. We had only a short time to crawl out the small window where the coal entered the coal house.

The coal we climbed over became a towering mountain. We pushed and pulled each other bravely up that mountain, stopping only to collect the gold that we had careful chipped off the coal. This gold was to be used to feed our families when we were in hiding. My stomach still feels the excitement and anxiety that we might be discovered and whisked off to prison.

Every once in a while we'd have to leave the outhouse section and hide when someone needed to use the outhouse. Donna would grab her baby, throw a blanket over its head and whisper, "Follow me, quick, I hear the Nazis coming." Mindless of pain, we crawled up the coal mountain, then out the window to hide in the deep ditch behind the buildings.

Sometimes we used the outhouse seat for a table or stove to serve or cook our imaginary food. Occasionally, a wasp would fly in and send us to the coal house until his tenancy was up.

I don't remember a bad odor in the outhouse because Aunt Da and Uncle Roy, who reared us, kept white quick lime inside the holes.

When I was about eleven years old, they tore the outhouse and coal house down and built a tool shed and chicken house combination. Somehow the indoor plumbing never achieved the excitement that the outhouse and the coalhouse did.

I've been in more modern outhouses before but never again have I read the funny papers on the wall while I sat on the pot with dishpan diarrhea. Of course, this ploy, played out by thousands of kids who were told to do the dishes, seldom worked. No matter how much we suffered from this affliction, when we entered the kitchen trying to appear pale and sickly, we discovered the dishes waiting with hardened food stuck on them like cement.

It's strange how a building could be so secure during the day and so fearful at night. Perhaps even God enjoyed seeing two little girls learn to love and protect their families by playing house in the outhouse.

THE PANTY CAPER

By Barbara Hostetler

When I was a little girl living in the big city, I knew nothing about outhouses until we visited my aunt and uncle on the farm. Indoor plumbing had not yet reached into the farming community in which they lived.

I was fascinated by the mysterious outhouse. It was a dark place with rough wooden walls and wooden seats worn smooth by many a derriere. I looked fleetingly down into the hole before proceeding with the business at hand, wondering just where this place led. It was such a dark, seemingly bottomless, pit.

One day, the questions I was harboring got the best of my five-year-old mind, and in an attempt to determine how deep it was, I dropped my white panties down into the abyss. I don't remember what my reaction was to the depth, but I do remember the response I received from my mother. All she said was, "Oh, for heaven's sake, Barbara! Why on earth did you do that?!"

Mom's Victorian English upbringing saved me from being chastised in the car on the long trip home in the presence of my dad and brothers. That would never have been discussed in mixed company...not even *private* mixed company.

TURTLE IN THE OUTHOUSE

By Rev. James C. Hefley

With Shep and Danny Boy trooping behind us, we headed for the barn to get Ole Timbrook, Daddy's breed stallion. On the way we passed Daddy's dog lot where he was feeding his bluetick coonhounds.

"Whar ya boys goin'?"

"Mama said we could go fishin'," Fesser said.

By the time we got to the sandbar, the sun had gone down over the bluff and the shadows were creeping in from the woods behind us. A throaty bullfrog harrumphed from the water's edge at the bluff. I shone the flashlight across to try and see him. Fesser grabbed my hand. "Douse that light, Monk. You'll scare the fish."

My rod twitched. I felt a steady pull. "Somethin's takin' my minner," I squealed. "Hit's running toward the bluff."

"Easy, easy. Let 'em run with it," Fesser counseled. "Let 'em swallow the bait. Then set the hook."

I gave it two or three feet of line, then jerked back. "I've got hit, Fesser. I've got me a big 'un. My pole's bent plumb to the water. Help me out, Fesser. I cain't reel hit in! This derned ole fish's gonna pull me right in the hole."

Fesser grabbed ahold of my rod. He couldn't budge the creature.

"That ole fish is gonna break my line. I'm goin' atter hit."

"Don't jump in the water, Monk." Fesser's call came too late. I already had a hand on the line and was wading into the deep water. I could feel something big and heavy pulling. It didn't seem to be a bass, for a bass would have jumped and tried to throw the hook, I figured.

I ducked my head under the surface and felt something rough with my hands. I came up sputtering.

"Fesser, I've got a snappin' turtle as big as the bottom of a warsh tub! He's got his feet down in the mud. I'll try to lift his hind end and you reel 'em in from the front."

I ducked under the water again, grabbed the turtle by its tail and pulled. I came up for air and went down again. The turtle's hind feet broke free of the mud.

Fesser pulled the turtle's front feet up and started reeling the critter in. I dipped down and pushed the turtle forward as its tail flipped above the surface.

Danny Boy jumped in the creek and grabbed a hind foot of the turtle. The turtle spurted forward. Shep was barking his head off. Fesser staggered back and pulled the turtle into the shallow water. I came splashing after it.

"Get the toesack, Monk. I'll hold the turtle."

Danny Boy turned loose of the turtle's leg and snapped at its head. "Get back, pup. You'll get your nose bit off," Fesser hollered.

Reeling harder, Fesser pulled the mossback on to the dry sandbar.

"Hold the sack open, Monk. I'm gonna ease 'em into it."

Fesser pulled that old turtle's head into the mouth of the sack and his rear in with his foot. Then he cut my line and tied the sack so the turtle couldn't get out.

I danced around the sack. "That's the biggest dadgummed turtle I ever seed, Fesser. Hit's worth more than a barrel of ole bass. Mama'll cook hit up 'n we'll eat fer a week."

"If we can only get it home," Fesser said. "That thing must weigh 40 or 50 pounds. Too heavy for me to carry all the way there."

"We've gotta git 'em up on old Timbrook, Fesser. We jist gotta."

Fesser brought Ole Timbrook over to the sandbar and lifted me up on the horse's back. Then he hoisted the sack containing the turtle as high as he could and I reached down to pull it up on the stallion. I'd never lifted anything that heavy.

Timbrook whinnied and reared up. One of his front feet almost came down on Danny Boy. I dropped the sack with the turtle in it onto the sandbar and grabbed a fistful of Timbrook's mane as the horse shot out toward the woods. Fesser, Danny Boy and Shep came running after us. Timbrook ran under a tree. I grabbed a limb and the horse ran on, leaving me dangling in the air.

I hung there a second and then dropped down. Fesser corralled Timbrook and tied him up again. He shone the light on the big stallion and stepped back. "No wonder Timbrook ran, Monk. You would too if an old turtle had clawed yer side. What say we jist put that old turtle back in the creek," Fesser suggested.

I jumped straight up. "No sirree. I purt near got my neck broke 'cause of that ole turtle. I'm taking' 'em home fer Mama to cook, iffen I have ta drag 'em all the way."

My brother took his knife and cut off a big branch from a hickory tree. He poked the stick through the sack. "Okay, Monk, you grab one end and I'll take the other. We'll carry the turtle home."

We got home a little after 10 p.m. My arm felt like it was about to come off. The lights were out, but Mama had stayed awake as she always did when one of her kids was out at night. "Is that you, Howard Jean? Where's your big brother?"

"He went to take Timbrook to the barn."

"Did you catch any fish?"

"No, Mama."

"Then get your wet clothes off and come to bed."

"I'll be thar in a minute, Mama. I've gotta take care of Danny Boy."

I waited with Danny Boy and the turtle by the yard fence until Fesser came back.

"Where on earth are we gonna put the turtle, Monk?"

I had already thought of that. "We'll put 'em in the outhouse. Tie 'em up an shet the door. Then we'll git up real

28

early and git Daddy to help us kill and clean hit, so Mama kin cook hit up."

We carried the big snapper turtle down to the outhouse. Fesser cut a hole in the toesack and wrapped the turtle tightly with rope to keep it from crawling off. Leaving room for the head to stick out, he tied the critter just inside the outhouse door, so it wouldn't crawl up and fall into one of the holes. We closed the door and walked back to the house, tired to the bone.

The house grew quiet. Going to sleep was like falling off a cliff into a black hole.

The sounds and smells of Mama fixing breakfast and the voices of my twin sisters, Loucille and Louise, woke me the next morning. The girls were playing outside. I pushed back the window screen and dropped Danny Boy to the ground. Fesser kept right on snoring in the bed across the room.

I pulled on my overalls and shirt and walked barefoot into the kitchen. Jimmie and baby Freddie, were already banging their spoons on the table. "Mmmmmmmm, Mama. Shore smells good," I said. I had forgotten all about the turtle.

A little girl's wail came from down near the outhouse. "Mama! Mama!"

Mama jumped. "That's Loucille. She and Louise went to the toilet. I'd better go see what's wrong. They may have seen a snake. I told your daddy to clean out that weed patch by the outhouse. Watch the eggs. Keep an eye on Jimmie and Freddie."

It hit me just as Mama ran out the kitchen door. The turtle Fesser and I had carried home last night. The twins had stepped into the outhouse and seen him. Maybe he had bit Loucille.

I forgot all about the little kids at the table. I raced to wake up Fesser. "Git up!"

Fesser opened his eyes. Both twins were crying now.

"Air turtle may have got one of the twins, Fesser."

Fesser leaped out of bed and jumped into his overalls, without even bothering to grab a shirt. We rushed out of the house and ran toward the outdoor toilet.

Louise and Loucille were both crying. Danny Boy and Shep were barking. Mama was standing behind Loucille tugging at something. When we got closer, I saw Mama's face. I'd never seen it that white before.

Loucille was pumping her thin little legs like she was trying to run and couldn't. Danny Boy and Shep added to the racket, barking, growling and lunging in and out at the turtle behind Loucille.

Fesser and I skidded to a stop. We saw the problem. The doggoned turtle had broken Fesser's rope and grabbed hold of Loucille's dress and bloomers. Mama was trying to jerk my sister's clothes from the turtle's mouth. I remembered hearing one of the old men say on the store porch, "Don't ever let a turtle bite ya. Hit won't tarn loose til hit thunders." I looked up at the clear morning sky and shuddered.

Loucille was screaming. "Hit's gonna eat me. Git hit off me! Hurry, Mama! Hit's gonna eat me."

Fesser kicked the turtle under its shell. It pitched up and clunked back on the ground, but didn't turn loose.

I grabbed a broomstick and jabbed at the critter's mouth, once, twice, three times. I beat it over the head. "Dad-blamed critter, tarn ma sister loose!" I hit it again. It pulled back, releasing Loucille. Mama sprawled backward on the ground, and Loucille fell on top of her.

Fesser noosed the rope around the turtle's neck, just as it bit down on my broomstick. "Mama, we've got hit now," I yelled triumphantly.

Mama scrambled up and hugged Loucille to her legs. "You're all right, honey. That terrible creature can't hurt you now."

Mama glowered at me and Fesser. "What I want to know is how that turtle got into our toilet."

Fesser couldn't bear to look at Mama. My eyes darted from her to the turtle.

Mama put a heavy hand on my brother's shoulder. "Did you boys bring that turtle home from the creek last night?"

"Uh-huh," Fesser grunted.

"Mama, don't blame James. He wanted to put the turtle back in the creek. I dinged 'em ta bring hit home."

I began sobbing. "Mama, I figured you could cook that ole turtle 'n hit'd be enuff to feed us fer a whole week. Please don't tell Daddy to give us a lickin'. We didn't mean nuthin' wrong."

The girls had stopped crying. A grin spread across Mama's face.

"Mama, whut's so funny?" I asked.

"That ole turtle hangin' on to Loucille's dress and bloomers. Never saw anythin' like it."

Mama always was a softie. She slipped one arm around my shoulder and the other around Fesser's. "I don't reckon there's been any harm done. I know you boys meant well, but, Howard Jean, I can't cook that horny creature. I could boil it for a week and you still couldn't cut the meat with an ax. Go tie it up so won't get loose. Then come and get your breakfast. You can take it back to the creek after school this evening."

MORNING GLORY MEMORIES

By Katherine Ganschow

I was born in 1903. When I was a girl, we moved into a new home that Papa bought just off Main Street in Ohio, Illinois. Mama loved her new home, located right behind the Catholic church, with one exception. She had looked forward to a bathroom and an indoor toilet but this house had neither.

There were only two houses on the south side of the church, ours and the Anderson family's home. The Andersons were strangers to us, but became dear friends in a very short time. That's because midway between our home and the Anderson's were two outhouses, built two feet apart and just 50 feet from the public sidewalk that passed directly in front of our homes. That sidewalk crossed a narrow road used to reach Ohio's grade and high school building, so you can imagine how much traffic there was on that sidewalk in front of the two outhouses.

Luckily, a wooden crisscross, eight-foot enclosure was built around both outhouses because mother wasn't about to exhibit her coming and going to the outhouse for all to see. Shortly after we moved into our new home Mama talked with Mrs. Anderson and suggested that a crawling vine might distract observers from knowing what was actually behind the wooden crisscross structure. Mother's morning glories that climbed up that structure were beautiful - and the talk of the town.

During those years, the people in Ohio, Illinois, had never heard of toilet tissue. Why worry when Sears, Roebuck remembered everyone with its catalogs? The catalog paper during those days was a little more absorbent and less colorful than the catalogs of today.

Going to the outhouse in the summertime didn't bother us too much, but the wintertime was a different story. On cold, blustery days, we wore long, heavy underwear; heavy black stockings; and black shoes that buttoned five or six inches up the side. We had to use a silver tool to fasten the buttons. It wasn't much fun taking off coats and pulling down stockings and long underwear to do our business in the outhouse in the middle of winter.

For many years, Ohio had very few indoor toilets. So whenever we visited friends we were very observant of their outhouses. It became quite an accomplishment if enough wallpaper could be saved following a spring house papering to cover the inside walls of the outhouse to make it more pleasant. Mother decorated ours and it was beautiful. A basket was attached to the wall so the catalogs would not get soaked from the snow and rain that inevitably dripped in through the roof.

On Halloween night, teenage boys from Ohio and other surrounding towns thought it hilarious to tip over the outhouses. When daylight arrived, it was difficult to find one outhouse standing upright in the whole town.

All I can say is, we should all be glad we're living in the days of comfortable indoor plumbing.

FLAT IRON PARK'S MINIATURE TOWN

By Katie Harrington

During the 1920s, Rudie was a teenager. Although he was not mean spirited, he had a will of his own and loved pranks. Rudie's father, who was principal of the Wisconsin School for the Deaf in Delavan, wanted to be very sure his younger son did not disgrace the family by raising havoc in the community.

Rudie's parents tried to guide him toward loftier pursuits by punishment, reasoning and direct orders. Nothing seemed to work. As a small child Rudie's mouth was washed out with vile-tasting lye soap and he declared, "Mmmm, boy, that's good stuff!"

As a youth, Rudie and his friends tried to skate fast enough over the thin ice in the middle of the Mill Pond without breaking through. Adults warned them about the importance of having good sense while ice skating, but Rudie still broke through the ice on a number of occasions.

One particular Halloween evening, Rudie and his friends were looking for a good time. Many of the homes in Delavan had indoor plumbing but there were also still plenty of outhouses around.

Rudie and his friends were gone quite a while that evening and when he returned he was grilled by his father, who was determined that he would not be disgraced in front of the mayor and other prominent friends. "You're sure you didn't tip over any outhouses, young man?" Rudie's father grilled him that night.

"No, Pop," Rudie replied seriously. "We did not tip over any outhouses. We're too old for such childish pranks. I just fooled around with my buddies."

The next morning a teacher stopped in the principal's office. "Say, Paul," he chuckled. "Did you see Flat Iron Park this morning?"

Paul rushed to the lovely little park near St. Andrew's Catholic Church where townspeople often enjoyed the formal gardens. There he found neat rows of outhouses laid out like a miniature town. Each outhouse bore a well-crafted handmade sign. One was labeled "Doyne Rayne Lumber Company." Another, "Bradley Knitting Mill." The next, "Wisconsin State Bank." Even the "Wisconsin School for the Deaf" was included.

No one ever found out who all was responsible for Flat Iron Park's miniature town, but for weeks, childish smirks were hidden behind adultlike scowls on the faces of Rudie and his friends. Paul never knew for sure who was the city planner for Flat Iron Park Town, but he knew without a doubt that his son Rudie was one of the construction workers.

DISASTER IN THE OUTHOUSE

By Jeannine Miller

During my childhood, very few in our family owned a car and it was a special occasion when a relative visited and we were treated to an outing. My dear grandmother Ada and I both experienced car sickness many times.

I remember one particular outing that was very enjoyable, but upon returning home, grandmother Ada made a bee line to the outhouse, dragging me along by the hand. She immediately upchucked and then asked me if I would like to earn a dime. At that time, a dime was a fortune.

My fortune would be earned, grandmother said, by retrieving her dentures from the large hole in the outhouse. I accepted the job while she hung on tightly to the waist of my dress. Mission accomplished!

HORSEFLIES AND OTHER HORRORS

By Kay L. Pliszka

As I stood in line to use a public portable toilet at a city festival, my mind drifted back to my childhood and to the outhouse at my Uncle Larry's farm. I hated that outhouse! As a little girl, I would open the door slowly -- cautiously. It was sweltering inside...and dark...and smelly. Giant horseflies buzzed and swooped like dive bombers. A creepy crawler scooted across the wooden seat where I would soon have to place my bare bottom! Goodness knows what other sleazy insects might be underneath the perimeter of that open hole -- critters might very well tiptoe onto my little pink doomed derriere while I was in the process of doing my duty.

As the door slammed behind me, it took all the courage I could muster to finally assume that vulnerable position. With my feet dangling helplessly above the floor, my fear fantasies escalated to unbearable proportions. What if a hairy spider crept out from under the ledge to tickle my tender tush? What if a bee, once dormant below, suddenly swooped up to sting my soft little seat? What if there were a snake down there that would silently slither up the side of that cesspool to hiss on my tiny heinie?

Just then the door to the modern portable toilet opened and I snapped back to reality.

"That's it!" I exclaimed aloud. As everyone else in line turned to stare, I stepped out of line and explained, "I'm *not* going through that again!" And with that I walked off in a huff to look for my husband, knowing it was not going to be easy to convince him that we needed to go home earlier than expected.

Graffiti in the Outhouse

By Geri Reiman

When I was a kid, my friend Betsy and I went with her parents and brother to their lake cottage on Pickerel Lake in East Troy, Wisconsin. Betsy's parents had just installed a brand-new outhouse on their property. It was just too much for Betsy and me. Immediately we started to write all over the walls and I mean *all over the walls*. Our names were everywhere. We were so proud of our handiwork. We didn't say a word to her parents or brother. Nobody mentioned anything. By evening, we were actually disappointed that no one had seen or mentioned our artistic ability.

The next day, Betsy and I went to the outhouse. Something new had been added to our creative work. Betsy's brother had written in large letters where everyone would see it, "Fools' names like fools' faces always appear in public places. Signed: Billy."

FIRST TELLING

By Barbara Smith

Every once in a while, maybe a dozen times in your whole life, you own something that is really yours, something you know to have been tagged with your name long before time began, something that no one else in the whole universe in all of time could ever have owned.

Like the ring you saw in the Milwaukee store window, that monogrammed silver ring that you hinted for and left clues about and finally asked for. "It's the only thing I want in the whole world, Mama. I promise I won't ask for anything else."

And there it was on your tenth birthday, your round-faced mother so pleased with her gift, your lanky father pleased that you and she were so pleased. You pulled off the yellow ribbon and tore off the blue paper and opened the tiny white cardboard box, and there it was, the silver ring monogrammed with a gothic "B" a fancy initial that conveniently stood for both birthday and Barbara. It fit loosely on your left middle finger, loose, your mother explained, so that you could grow into it.

You spent that birthday on your grandfather's Illinois farm, hugging your tall, badly bent grandmother, who died the following September. You rode the truck when your florist uncle delivered sprays to the church for a wedding, and you rolled the dough when your aunt said to roll so that she and you could brag on your gooseberry pies, the pies you had asked for instead of a cake.

Late on that sticky afternoon, with the sun's hot kiss on the back of your neck, the blossoms dropping from the limbs of the peach tree, you had to go to the bathroom. Your grandfather did not believe in plumbing bills, so you and he and everyone else had to walk the narrow path past the gladioli and cabbages, the chicken yard and the pigpen, to the outhouse that had no crescent moon on the door. It had only plain old square windows high over your head so you couldn't look in or out. And you accomplished your purpose in spite of the atmosphere and in spite of the splinters and in spite of the bees whose sound filled you with terror. Then you ripped pages from the Sears, Roebuck catalog and used them as catalog pages were meant to be used. You dropped them down, down, deep into the hole, and you saw the glint of silver that went with them. And when you looked, your birthday finger was bare.

That beautiful ring had been made just for you, before trees, before time, before starlight began, and you couldn't even cry.

You had to fib about why the ring had disappeared, saying you had put it away until you grew into it. No one ever mentioned the ring again, but something that has never mended broke then inside of you and, until now, you have never told anyone.

BELL'S OWT HOUSE

By Maggie Windsor

Once upon a time in the days of yore, there was an outhouse. It stood resplendent at the end of our garden path, complete with half-moon and a coat of white paint. It was covered with ornamental vines of ivy of the ginseng family with evergreen leaves, yellowish flowers and black berries. The vines were my mother's idea; she didn't want the neighbors to know what it was. Alas, how could they not know? Theirs were identical except of course for the dazzling decorations. Also, the endless flow of family members--my grandmother Margaret, great-uncle Ted, my mother, my two brothers, two sisters and me--left no doubt of its use, for we traipsed up the path and back at all hours.

Inside this magnificent structure, also painted white, my mother had installed toilet seats over the two holes and placed the traditional Sears, Roebuck catalog equidistant between the places where we dropped anchor.

On busy days, my sister Betty and I would go together. I admit we overstayed the allotted time, but the Sears, Roebuck catalog fascinated us. We would sit and turn its pages and dream about the wondrous gowns and slippers and wish that we could have them. Where we thought we could wear them, I do not know; I was only certain that we should have them.

Our dear mother was on to our tricks. If she thought we had lingered beyond our time, she would toss tin cans with gusto against the outhouse door. Not one, but one after another. We'd be sitting there in our world of illusion and dreams, when suddenly, whang, whang, whang! We knew it was time to depart.

One day, Great-Uncle Ted, my mother and I were lined up with our reading material, waiting to go into the outhouse, and Betty took our picture. This was to impress us with the importance of shortening our visits. I'm sure that Great-Uncle Ted, who was known for extra-long visits himself, would not have stood still for the picture had he known what Betty was up to, but then Great-Uncle Ted's elevator did not always go to the top floor. He probably thought we were lined up just to have our picture taken. Poor soul, he was such a loving old man, and I know we teased him more than somewhat.

That photo did not shorten our visits, for we still lingered over the good old Sears, Roebuck, but it did give us a good addition to the family archives.

One Halloween, some of the revelers pushed over the elegant structure. In the morning when we looked out, there it was on its back, the two holes still standing sturdily. I would have sworn it was my brother and his pals who were responsible. It took some heavy equipment to get it upright. Across the front the pranksters had painted, **BELL'S OWT HOUSE**. We all looked and laughed, since getting people "owt" of the outhouse was Mother's constant campaign. That afternoon, Mother put us all to work cleaning the old thing. That "owt house" was, after all, a bright and shining moment in our lives.

HOW TO GET A NEW BATHROOM

By Jennie Whitmer

I came in on the bus from St. Louis and my cousin Posey picked me up at the store where the bus dropped and picked up passengers. He was sporting a 1940 Ford truck and was pretty proud of it. I was proud too, for it was about a five-mile walk out to the farm where my mother lived.

As soon as I walked in the house, I knew something was wrong. The tension was thicker than cream on top of a milk can. After supper Mr. Watts left to check on the calves he was bucket-feeding over at his farm and I asked Mom what was wrong.

"Well, honey, it's just that Arvil isn't exactly the person I thought he was when I married him."

"Then why don't you tell him to leave, Mom? This is your home. Let him go back to his place and call it quits."

Mother and Mr. Watts had been married for three years. As with most second marriages, there were some matters of convenience involved but the most important parts, like warmth and kindness and fun, were missing. I had noticed that before.

Mr. Watts farmed both his place and Mother's. When they married, he moved in with Mom in her house and rented out his own. Unfortunately his renter, a Mr. Finch, had passed away a short time after moving to the Watts' farm, leaving a lonely widow to mourn his passing and pay the rent as best she could.

Mother continued, "It's not quite that simple, dear. A few months ago, I agreed to mortgage this place so Arvil would have money to make improvements on the house and buy new equipment to work the farms. So far, the only improvement I've seen is that he's not here for meals much anymore. He's no company to me, but if he stops making the payments, I'll lose the farm and it's all I have."

As we pumped and carried water for the supper dishes, Mother told me the widow Finch had an electric pump and running water in her kitchen.

"Electric?" I asked in amazement.

"Yes. Arvil had the line run out far as his house. He said if the crop is good next year, he might have it run on out here."

It was bad enough that Mother had given up her freedom for an old penny-pinching, grouchy skirt-chaser, but now her equity was gone too.

Mom said the widow Finch was wearing a pink glow on her cheeks and a different hat to church practically every Sunday. She also had a new storm cellar and a screened-in porch. Heaven only knew what else Arvil had given her.

I was pretty sure I knew what else and the picture of that old goat and the widow Finch made me snort a laugh before I could stop it.

I was barely making enough money to get by, but I suggested to Mom that she come to St. Louis and live with me. I had a room with a fold-down bed and I got to share the bathroom and kitchen with the owners and the other tenants.

"No, honey. Thanks for the offer, but I'm just going to let this ride for a while and if things don't get better on their own, I'll think of something."

My cousin Posey was coming to take me to the store so I could catch the bus back to the city. I needed to visit the little outhouse out back one more time before I left. Hollyhocks and larkspur stood guard next to it's weathered whitewashed walls. Sunlight falling through the gaps warmed the bench. Our outhouse was always clean. You could count on that as well as you could plenty of fresh air out on the farm. It wasn't a bad place, just freezing cold when the sleety wind howled. And it was rather unhandy when the curse was on you. Just before I started back up the path, I poured lime down the hole, using the old granite pan

Mom kept in the lime bag. It kept the smell down and made things look better too.

The next time I came home, it was fall and the leaves were all different colors. Mr. Watts had flown the coop not long after my previous visit. Shortly after that, Mother told the widow Finch that it was time for her to move on too. And since the Watts house was fixed up so much better than hers, Mom decided to move over there and sell her old place. She wanted to get moved and settled before winter set in and I'd come to help.

"Mom, where do you think Mr. Watts is? I sure hope he doesn't take a notion to come back." I couldn't imagine the old scudder leaving such a good setup, but I was glad he left and glad Mom was moving. She'd worked hard all her life and deserved a nice place to live.

"Honey, Arvil said many times to me, and anybody else that would listen, he'd rather be anywhere than stuck here with me. So I'm sure wherever he is, he's satisfied. He won't be back."

The man who ran the store told me earlier that he figured Mr. Watts and the widow Finch were somewhere together. He said he figured it was the best thing that ever happened to Mom.

The next day was moving day so Mother and I prepared to retire early. Posey was coming out in the morning to help us.

Naturally, I had to go down the outhouse path before I hit the sack. Purple asters, heavy with bloom, bowed low beside the door. From the pit beneath the bench, a thick layer of lime gleamed in the deepening twilight. A chill wind whipped through the cracks and there was a strong updraft. I noticed the pit was getting pretty full but no matter. After tomorrow, we would be using the flush toilet in Mr. Watts' house. He had built a bathroom and installed a fancy porcelain toilet stool not too long before he disappeared.

Mom said she thought if she had a bathroom put in her old house it would help sell it and I sure agreed with that. Mr. Watts had left a strongbox full of money besides what he had in the bank, so Mother, still being the old geezer's wife, was not going to hurt financially.

Our little outhouse had served us long and well but it would soon be just a memory. I was halfway to the big house when I decided to go back and dump the rest of that 50 pounds of lime into the pit. I also decided when Posey showed up in the morning, the first thing we ought to do was get the shovels and fill up that old pit. In fact, I thought we might as well tear down the outhouse and smooth the ground. We could plant some flower seeds. They'd be waiting under a nice bed of leaves, ready to spring up next year when the snow melted, the ground warmed and Mr. Watts was only a faded memory.

SHELTER FROM THE STORM

By Mary Fenlason

In the 1940s, there were no motels in our part of the country, just tourist cabins, mostly small boxy wooden structures at the side of the road. Some are still visible today, weathered and leaning over. The paths in the back of the cabins leading to the outhouses are no longer trod.

It was a great advantage to find a tourist cabin site located close to and upwind from the outhouse facilities, especially in July and August. This made for shorter walks in the middle of the night.

There were rules to follow, however. Wear your shoes, carry a flashlight, check the floor for snakes and beware of skunks and porcupines.

In the '70s when our children were old enough to see the country, we went first class with a camper on wheels. Again the rules applied for the site because our camper had all the comforts of home except one--there was no bathroom.

Our maiden trip was to a state park in a deep valley in southeastern Minnesota - Beaver Creek Valley. There was running water - a clear, clean, watercress-filled brook; tall basswood and ash trees for shade; and a spot right across the road from the communal outhouse.

It was a hot July afternoon when the sky turned a greenish color and the clouds had an ominous look to them. A neighboring camper told us that a year earlier when a storm came through their campsite, it took the ranger an hour to free two people from a crushed camper that looked just like ours.

At that moment we dashed across the street and found shelter in the outhouse, just a whiff a way from a close encounter with a twister. Though fragile and not too fragrant, that old outhouse was our haven from the storm.

THE FRIGHTENED FELINE

By Julie G. DeGroat

A chipmunk hurtled out of the bird feeder with our cat, Teacup, close behind. Teacup never caught any of those bothersome pests, but she never tired of perfecting her "pursuit and capture" techniques. Suddenly, the chipmunk cut to the left and scampered up the opened door of our old outhouse. Teacup, concentrating hard on pursuit technique, thought her prey had gone into the outhouse. She was probably thrilled to have cornered one at last.

I watched, waiting for Teacup to stalk out of the empty outhouse, pretending she'd meant to let the chipmunk go all along. She didn't appear. Curious, I left the kitchen and looked in the outhouse. No cat.

Had I somehow missed her exit? I'd just about decided I had, when I heard a muffled meow. I peered down the hole. Teacup crouched miserably on a narrow ledge halfway between the seat and the bottom. I reached one arm down, thinking to grab her, but she was too far away. I called her, hoping she could jump up and out, but she refused to budge.

My children heard the commotion and crowded into the narrow outhouse to offer advice.

"Dangle a hot dog in front of her and she'll jump out."

"Call the emergency operator!"

"Get Dad to come home from work."

My toddler, teetering precariously near the hole, started to cry. "I want my kitty!"

I shooed them all out and pondered the situation. The cat wouldn't jump out on her own. I couldn't reach her; my arms weren't long enough. Besides, what if I dislodged her and she fell into the pit...a pit better left *undescribed*?

I stuck a long board into the hole. I figured she could jump onto the board and crawl out. Not Teacup. That would have been too easy. Instead of using the board as an escape route, she viewed it an enemy, and did her best to avoid contact. Even Teacup's favorite treat, a cold hot dog, couldn't lure her up the board.

OK, time for plan number two...except that I didn't have another plan. I contemplated which child I could convince to let me fasten a rope around and send down the hole, but finally had to give that up as a bad idea.

"I guess she'll have to stay there until Dad gets home," I said. "I don't know what else to do!" Teacup's plaintive meows echoed eerily up from the toilet seat.

"Cut a hole in the outhouse and get her out," my daughter suggested.

About that time, I was ready to try anything, even sawing through the two-by-four framing construction. I got a handsaw from the shed. The only problem was, where to cut? I could remove the toilet seat easily, but if I tried to cut straight down, it would wrench the outhouse. To saw into the side was impossible, not to mention dangerous to the cat.

"Mom, you have to get her out," my daughter said. The other kids yelled, "Hurry, she's dying, get her out!"

Frustrated, I said, "Fine! Fine! Any bright ideas? What do you want me to do, lift the outhouse right off her?"

"Yes," said my toddler.

"Well, Mommy can't," I said. "I'm not strong enough to..." I paused. Hmmm. I couldn't lift the outhouse off the foundation, but maybe I could prop it up enough for her to crawl out.

I found a pry bar and a cinder block in the shed and stuck the bar under one edge of the outhouse. With a wrenching groan, it raised about an inch, but not enough even for a sneaky cat like Teacup to ease under.

"Come on, help me," I said. "We have to get this raised up."

The kids piled onto the prybar with more enthusiasm than skill. The outhouse majestically rose, teetered, then toppled onto the grass.

Teacup blinked twice, stepped delicately from the rim of the exposed pit, and sauntered off.

I'd like to say the cat learned her lesson and never chased another chipmunk. Unfortunately, there is no happy cat-loves-chipmunk ending. However, I would be willing to bet she never chased one anywhere near an outhouse again.

YE OLD BACK HOUSE

By Earle Hawke

Most people are not old enough to know much about back houses. We called them back houses because they were always in the back of the big main house. Another feature of the back house was that the door always swung in instead of out, and many times it saved our minds a lot of doubt. You could also put one foot against the door and be selective, at least for a few minutes, about who you would allow to come in with you.

After all, it was a two-holer. Some of the rich people had three-holers and toilet tissue, but we had Montgomery Ward and Sears, Roebuck catalogs and we usually got to the harness section about the first of May. Of course, we also had corn cobs as a last resort, both brown and white.

Back houses were always built a little on the forward slant so the door would stay shut by itself. Imagine trying to train eight kids to keep the back house door shut. It would also keep rodents and snakes from coming in, but once in a while if the wind blew in the right direction, a garter snake would come and the door would close and it couldn't get out. The next person to use the facility would get the dickens scared right out of him.

We also tipped over many back houses at Halloween time. I still don't know why we did a dumb thing like that, maybe because we weren't into heinous crimes back then as much as we are now, and we thought we needed something to do, like sneak around in the dark of night and do something naughty and not get caught. Whee!

This is the only time I have ever written anything about toilets of any kind, and I hope it's the last.

THE MURDO OUTHOUSE

By Steve Boehrer

In the summer of 1972, my wife, Rita, and I decided to take a short vacation to Yellowstone National Park. We were sick of the city and we needed some fresh air. Now, I haven't taken a poll to see if my experience is shared by others, but vacations bind me up. Maybe it's due to all that sitting time in an automobile. Maybe it's lacking the cozy comfort of my own crapper where the wallpaper design usually jump-starts peristalsis. Whatever the cause, when I go on vacation my peristalsis takes one also. It shifts to neutral. On this occasion, it had anticipated the vacation and came to a dead stop nearly a week before our departure.

We left work on a Friday evening and drove west from Milwaukee through Wisconsin. We stayed that night at the home of my wife's mother, Beryl, in the state's coulee region. By this time, my stomach had mutated to a compressor. Beryl made pies like no one else and that evening I stuffed more food into the compressor. My dear wife, not generally known as a "flannel mouth," let it be loudly known at the dinner table that I was suffering from...dum de dum dum...CONSTIPATION.

The next morning as we were about to drive away, Beryl reached through the open car window and handed me a large bag of pitted prunes.

"Munch on these," she said.

"Thanks, Beryl," I mumbled back.

We set Rapid City, South Dakota, as our destination for that day. I drove into Minnesota, munching. I munched as I listened to Rita. She read from our AAA Tour Book of the many charms about cities like Austin, Albert Lea, Fairmont and Worthington.

"Did you know that...?" she would say.

"No, really? Mmmmmm." Munch, munch.

I munched prunes as we entered South Dakota. Rita took over the driving and I kept on munching. I left the prunes in the car as we toured the Corn Palace at Mitchell and discovered the 1001 ways that corn can be both construction material and decor. I started munching again as soon as we left the Corn Palace and munched as we drove until the bag of prunes was empty...not too many miles past Mitchell.

We had intended to take the thirty-four mile drive through the Badlands on our way into Rapid City. Prune power intervened. As we entered the outskirts of Murdo, South Dakota, at 6:00 p.m. my insides suffered an implosion. Peristalsis awoke! It found speech! "Mayday! Mayday! Emergency! Delay is not acceptable! Right now! Mayday! Mayday! Now! Now! Now!"

I saw the little building at the side of the road in a small park. *God bless the Murdo Park District*, I thought as I screeched to a halt and vaulted out of the car.

"I'll see you when I see you," I yelled to Rita as I hobbled cross-kneed to the outhouse. It was a two-holer. There wasn't time for a critical selection. I lunged for the nearest seat. Relief surged forth. Dusk came. I saw it through the quarter moon cut above the door. The sun went down. I sat there, surging intermittently. It was black outside. Then the moon came up. The sky had brightened. I sat there. For awhile I was afraid I'd see sunup through that quarter-moon. Rita tells me that the smile I wore when I came out of that outhouse put that quarter-moon to shame.

I'm a lot older now. And BMs take on a whole new meaning and value as we age and our pleasures get simpler. In my house, an exceptional BM now goes by the name of *MURDO*. "I just had a *MURDO*" can set up a whole day, and carry the memory of a special outhouse through a lifetime.

BIGFOOT IN THE OUTHOUSE

By Alice Zillmer

Dad burst in the cabin door yelling. "Harold claimed he saw Bigfoot." Before Mother or I could say a word, Dad began throwing gear in a knapsack. Compass. Camera. Flashlight. First aid kit. A box of raisins and two bandoliers of 30-06 bullets. "Harold said Bigfoot broke into a small cabin somewhere near here. Saw him clawing on the siding. It sounded like Ike Wilke's place."

Dad's knapsack now bulged with a thermal blanket, field glasses, waterproof matches, toilet paper, laxatives and a Bible. Few assembly lines could match his packaging speed.

"Harold said he ran for his life," Dad added. "He snagged his pants, tore his suit coat and was stung, scratched and bit. But he made it back to the car."

It seems my cousin Harold and his wife, while visiting Wisconsin, had tried to locate Dad's new hunting camp. Afraid the narrow roads would do harm to their new car, Harold set off on foot.

"Where is Harold now?" mother asked. Mother had looked forward to having company while Dad and I bow hunted.

"I offered to drive 'em here, but they flat refused."

"Doesn't Bigfoot live in Tibet? Or the Utah mountains? How'd he get to Wisconsin?" I asked.

"Beats me. But Harold is a deacon at his church and not given to lying. And he swore the thing had huge hairy legs, oversized feet, a white underbelly and the eyes of a vulture."

"Aw, Harold saw a bear," I said. "Can't he tell a bear from Bigfoot?"

"I thought that too. But he swore the thing he saw had a multicolored feathered tail."

"A feathered tail?" I said trying to picture a yeti with tail feathers. Since when did abominable snowmen have tails?

"Maybe Harold's glasses steamed up," Mother said, trying to get her cousin Harold off the hook.

"Take care of your mother," Dad said. "I aim to get a look at this creature."

Dad's knapsack appeared stuffed, but he still found room for a sheathed machete in case of a hand-to-hand battle. He also squeezed in toothpicks, toenail clippers and a pocket dictionary. When it came to being prepared, Dad could give the head of the Boy Scouts what for.

Dad checked the safety on his 30-06, hoisted the knapsack and disappeared into the darkness.

Dad's new hunting camp in Bayfield County contained all I needed to keep Mother safe from abominable animals. That summer Dad built the one-room 'cabin using green poplar logs. A barrel stove provided heat. A two-burner kerosene stove served for cooking. Two gasoline lanterns, for light.

A hand pump installed inside next to a salvaged sink coughed up clear water. Two double bunk beds heavy with quilts guaranteed warm sleep. The nearby spring cooled butter and milk. A sunken watertight box kept bacon and pork chops from turning green. A two-seat outhouse built to withstand nature's most vicious weather -- so the donor said -- was delivered the day I arrived for opening of bow hunting season.

Why the outhouse ended up being the first building to greet a visitor's eye can be explained. The outhouse was offered as a gift. They say don't look a gift "house" in the mouth. Dad hadn't. My parents were in town when the gift arrived. The donor backed his flatbed truck into the drive. He and his cronies deposited the outhouse dead center. Delivery completed, they slunk off.

I arrived from Milwaukee as my parents returned from town. Dad's face registered dismay at seeing the outhouse. "Why'd they leave 'er here? Couldn't they see the two empty 55-gallon drums I buried behind the cabin?" he asked. "But I guess we can jockey 'er out back."

But Dad hadn't looked inside. The corner studs were solid oak six by sixes. The siding, floor and roof boards consisted of two-inch slabs of pine. The doors on the Fort Knox vaults weighed less than the door on that edifice. But the door swung freely thanks to three iron hinges secured by eighteen formidable bolts. Ventilation didn't come from some tacky half-moons. No sir. This gem had two tiny crank-open louvered windows. If anybody ever took to measuring and weighing outhouses for prizes, Dad had in his possession Academy Award material.

In the short time since the outhouse arrived, it seemed to have hunkered down about six inches into the gravel driveway.As the weight of the job ahead also began to sink in, Dad said, "I'd like to get my hands on the bruisers who delivered this thing. I'd lay 'em low in a hurry."

Dad clenched his fists and ground his dentures free of a year's tartar. Before long he began to laugh and said, "On the other hand, I'm no fool. There had to be a passel of them. So here she'll sit."

Relieved, Mother and I joined in his laughter. When it came to fisticuffs, Dad was about as schooled as Mother Theresa.

In some ways, Dad had it coming. His superb hunting and fishing skills was matched by uncanny luck. Even in down years, his game bag would be filled on opening day. But trouble came because he wasn't above rubbing it in. If his yarns were merely far-fetched, they wouldn't have rankled so much. But his feats were usually witnessed. The lads aimed the outhouse caper to even up the score.

Fortunately, Dad wasn't one to hold a grudge. (Or one to change his ways, either.)

The night he left to look for Bigfoot, Mom and I played cribbage by lantern light until 10 p.m. Just before bedtime, I cautiously flashed a light outside and headed for the outhouse. I slapped at a mosquito bent on tasting my cheek. It felt good to be free of the camouflage face paint I'd worn all day bow hunting, but I missed the mosquito repellent the paint contained. Whereas Dad shaved haphazardly, I had the whitest of faces and scrawniest of pale necks. For me, the brown, green and black face paint was a must.

I sat with the outhouse door open. For some reason Dad had half-filled the pails under the two outhouse seats with lime. Earlier in the day I mistakenly shut the door. The fumes from the lime and ammonia almost decked me. With my brown insulated underwear and camouflage hunting pants down hugging my knees, I was handicapped. Opening the door required both hands. I hobbled out and clung to the building until my dizziness passed. I wheezed, trying to fill my lungs with untainted air. Using baby steps to re-enter, I recall collapsing on the seat – but with the door wide open. Eyes watering freely, I stared down the driveway and couldn't help admiring what I presumed to be a wild rose bush in full flower along the road.

My – ah – task finally completed, I remember standing and hoisting up underwear and hunting pants. Last I buckled on my belt complete with a full quiver of colorfully fletched hunting arrows that bounced along my backside. My eyes were still watering from the lime fumes, but I thought I saw the rose bush fly off into the woods.

Oh, oh! Wait a minute. We heard that since Cousin Harold became a deacon, he'd taken to wearing big-and-tall-men's polyester suits when he passed the collection plate. Could the rose bush have been Cousin Harold wearing one of his flamboyant purchases? The first time Mother saw my camouflage face paint, it unnerved her plenty. Her family leaned toward flightiness.

I decided to tell Mother the Bigfoot mystery was solved. When Dad returned, I'd tell him, too – if he wasn't too spent.

But I'd balk at telling Cousin Harold. My big feet had always been an embarrassment to me. And my baggy hunting pants could have made my legs look big and furry from a distance. It all made perfect sense, especially with my hunting arrows dangling behind. But I still wasn't going to tell Harold -- because I'd be doggone if the main topic for merriment at every future family reunion was going to be my white underbelly.

HALLOWEEN FUN
1930'S STYLE

By Gene Tuma

Tipping over a neighbor's outhouse on Halloween night was a thrill enjoyed by many boys living on a farm in the 1930s. I remember one year when good ole Mr. D's outhouse was on the hit list. (I can't identify Mr. D since his kin may still be looking for the culprits who did this dastardly deed.)

It seems that Mr. D had responded to Mother Nature's call and he was sitting quietly on the throne when the well-planned trick took place. Of course the evildoers did not know or at least did not care that Mr. D was inside his outhouse. They also did not realize when they did the tipping that the door to the outhouse was facing the ground.

None of the perpetrators stayed around long enough to hear poor Mr. D's cry, "Let me out!" Not a soul in Mr. D's home heard his cry either since the outhouse was a good number of yards away from the house. It wasn't until milking time came around early the next morning that the family finally heard the now-faint call, "Please, please, someone get me out of here!" With much grace and I'm sure with some snickering taking place, Mr. D. was finally rescued from his outhouse prison.

THE HERMANS - - ONE AND TWO

By Virginia Rudasill Mortenson

Mama, Daddy, two-year-old George, and I, Virginia Lee, aged seven, moved to Four-Mile in 1946. My parents knew nothing about the area of Des Moines, Iowa, called Four-Mile when they moved into the Camp Dodge house.

Camp Dodge, a military camp on the outskirts of Des Moines, used the small makeshift buildings as temporary barracks during World War II when the camp trained more new recruits than it could handle in the camp's permanent bunks. After the war the three-room boxes were carted into neighborhoods that wouldn't squawk too loud about their unsightliness.

Mama and Daddy didn't care what the house had been before. Daddy had come home from the war, and they wanted a house of their own. No more apartment living for them. The American dream. Their own home. Even if they had to go into debt $2,500. Even if the house had only one bedroom with no door. Even if the house had no basement, no attic and no running water. Even if the house had no indoor bathroom.

In the beginning, I loved the tiny house. With its glitzy, yellow fake-brick siding I thought it looked like a fairy house. I'd press my nose against the roughness of the bricks to see the sparkle of metallic flakes up close. Not only that, but a blanket of bright green grass spread out forever, actually an acre, with just a few bumps to mar the smoothness: a grape arbor, plum and peach trees, and our own rhubarb patch beside a hill topped by a silver water pump.

With several leaps over the garden I could be stirring up the dust, sliding down the bank to the creek. Our very own

Four-Mile Creek. Who can describe the joy of possessing a muddy shoreline, bubbly creek water and all the rocks, bugs and frogs a girl could ask for?

The creek was wonderful but, as strange as it seems, when I was seven, one of the real delights for me was Herman, our very own outhouse. We called our outhouse Herman because when someone needed to visit the outhouse in the middle of a Monopoly game or during dinner, he or she announced, "I'll be right back. I have to go visit Herman."

For a girl who liked to daydream and make up poems and sing ridiculous songs at the top of her lungs, Herman provided a safe place to be alone. No critics sat beside me in the outhouse. At night, Herman transformed into a study where composition radiated possibilities. Pure quiet reigned. Only the moonlight squeezed in through the many cracks in the unpainted boards.

"Phew! How can you stay in there so long? You're weird," my brother said often as he grew older.

"Better be here than anywhere near you. Smells better too!" I always flipped back.

Of course, Halloween was the favorite time for the neighborhood boys to push over the outhouses. Herman, being especially old and flimsy, practically shouted out, "Me! Me! Push me over. I'm easy!"

The neighborhood rowdies complied, until one year Daddy announced that enough was enough. "A new outhouse - - Herman Number Two is coming. Those boys'll play heck tipping her over."

Why Daddy called the new outhouse a her and still called *her* Herman I never understood. Maybe, because the word *Herman* started with a *her*?

"Isn't she a beauty?" Daddy blushed as the big white mausoleum of an outhouse dropped into place over the two buried barrels. "Look! She's a two-seater!"

We all nodded to please Daddy, and really, truly Herman Number Two did outshine every other outhouse in Four-

Mile. Way too solid to tip over. In fact, so solid that no moonlight danced through any cracks. No cracks whatsoever in the smooth white boards.

Poor Herman Number One got his bottom sawed off to make a playhouse for George and his little friend Mary Lou. Glowing in green jealousy, I teased the two unmercifully. Mama always said I'd get paid back for teasing my brother. I guess I did, too.

One night I woke up knowing I had to visit Herman Two. I stumbled out the back door to float over the long acre of grass, almost all the way to the creek. Without being fully awake, I squeaked open the door, my eyes still almost closed.

But, later, when I finished my business and tried to push the door to leave, it refused to budge. I knocked a few times, polite, against Herman Two's tight boards. The darkness enveloped me like chocolate surrounding the marshmallow inside a Mallo Cup candy bar. If only the smell had been as sweet.

My heart thumped inside my skinny chest underneath my flannel nightie. I pounded the door not so timidly now. Fully awake, my eyes probably looked like neon green floodlights.

"Help! Help! Mama! Daddy!" I began to cry. I could spend the rest of my life inside the bowels of Herman Two or at least until someone else in the family had to pay a visit. Probably, at least until morning. And would I still be alive by then?

I could imagine the blackness not as mere air but dense with squashed-together bogeymen. Bogeymen who smelled!

My entire body thickened into a battering ram. I banged myself against the door, screaming at the top of my lungs, not caring if I hurt my head, hands or body. Being bruised was better than being dead.

Suddenly, Herman Two's side flew open to moonlight and lilac-scented air. Mama's face scrunched into a half-smile. She asked, "What in tarnation?"

"You, you...opened the side?..." I stuttered.

"Don't you remember, honey? Herman Two faces a different way. This is the door."

Relief flushed through me as I stumbled from Herman Two. I circled Mama's softness with my arms. Her robe smelled like cocoa and Camay soap.

Mama's body started to jiggle, and then it shook as she erupted into full-blown laughter. I began laughing too, laughing so hard, tears filled my eyes. And as I looked through the blur, I'm almost positive that I saw Herman Two laughing with us.

STOP, I GOTTA GO!

By V. Catherine Kozij

I walked with great sadness across the lawn where the frame house once stood, the frame house that had withstood decades of life since the Great Depression. The scorched meadow was fresh. Charred grass crunching beneath my white athletic shoes, shattered glass bottles, a bent pipe and an empty canning jar were all symbolic of the house that once stood proudly on this spot.

Suddenly, a belch of dust billowed in front of me and blew into my eyes. I coughed, rubbed my eyes and knocked off my glasses in the process. When I squinted and looked again, the setting had returned to our old neighborhood we'd known as children in the early 1960s. There in front of me was the house that belonged to the family with seven children. Behind the house and up the hill a bit was the two-seater outhouse.

The outhouse, once a sturdy sentinel, shone its sleek roof at the sky, wearing it like a pretentious uniform hat. The door, splintered but solid, held its secrets tight to its chest like a seasoned gambler with a winning deck of cards.

Suddenly, someone came out from behind the outhouse. "Hey, Rogerstein," a boy said laughing.

It made me blink. "Who are you?" I asked, trying hard to identify the voice.

"Don't you remember me?"

I could hear the smile in his voice.   "You sound like…Oh! Could it be? Daniel?"

"Yeah," he laughed, "Who else calls you Rogerstein?"

"Just your sister," I said.

The outhouse door slammed as a girl bounded out. "Hi, Rogerstein!" she called out and laughed. "Still blind without your glasses, huh?"

"Darla!" I gasped. "How many years has it been?"

She scratched her head. "What are you talking about, Rogerstein? It's only been since this morning."

The door slammed once again. Out came my best friend and schoolmate, Beth. "Last one to the car's a rotten egg," she said as she ran down the hill.

I gasped as I realized we were eleven years old again.

"I'll drive," Darla yelled out.

"You always drive," Beth said.

It's my car," Darla reminded her.

"Our car," corrected Daniel. He was one of Darla's five brothers.

We ran for the front seat of the incapacitated 1948 Buick convertible sitting under the trees. It hadn't started its life as a convertible but, after an attempt to pass a trailer of freshly picked oranges by going underneath, it became a roofless vehicle. The smell of oranges remained in the upholstery. Five years ago, Mr. Barrett had packed it under the oaks and let us kids "drive" it. We shared the space with the trees, the raccoons and the occasional mama cat and her kittens.

We three girls jumped into the front seat and slammed the door. We could just as easily have jumped into the seats by climbing over the edge of the car. There was no need to buckle our seat belts either. There weren't any. Besides, we weren't going anyplace anyway. Mr. Barrett had sold the motor parts for scrap years ago.

"Pull over to the side," Beth said. "I gotta go." She climbed over the edge of the abandoned vehicle, taking leaves and dirt with her. The shelter of the trees made a mess of the seats as did the birds. But it was a cool break from the hot, summer sun.

Beth headed for the wooden outhouse and closed the door hanging on its hinges. Her small fingers wrapped around the edges of the splintered wood and squeezed it shut. "I can't go and hold the door at the same time," she yelled from inside.

"No one is going to watch you," Darla said.

"I can't go. It stinks in here," Beth shouted as she hopped off the seat.

Beth climbed back into the car. "Drive me to the next toilet," she said. I want one that doesn't stink as much as that one."

Darla beamed, "As soon as Reverend Samuels gets more wood, he's going to start building our new house."

"Gonna have a bathroom in it?" Beth asked.

"Yep," Darla said proudly.

"Hurry up," Beth said, "I really gotta go."

"You always gotta go," Daniel told her.

Just then another dust devil whirled by. I blinked my eyes and remembered the day, almost 30 years earlier, when we kids watched in sadness as construction workers pulled off the roof and then tore down the splintery walls of that shabby outhouse. Next, they shoveled sand into the holes until it was no more than a level place in the dirt.

I smiled as I stood there, because it was still easy to find the spot where that old outhouse had provided many a childhood memory. Not far up from the scorched meadow below where the frame house once stood, was a patch of the healthiest, greenest, thickest grass I'd ever seen. Well-fertilized grass, to be sure.

FRENCH LICK'S ELITE OUTHOUSES

By Katie Harrington

In the early 1900s French Lick, Indiana, was an exclusive resort for the very wealthy who went there to bathe in the therapeutic hot springs and to drink the restorative waters. Rich patrons came from Chicago and spent weeks in the luxurious rooms, dining in the gourmet dining room under imported light fixtures and walking over beautifully manicured lawns and among the marble columns. This was high society at its most elegant.

French Lick was a small town and most of the people depended upon the resort for their very existence. Therefore each guest was treated like a king or queen.

A row of elegant outhouses stood behind the hotel. At the beginning of a stay at the posh resort, all genteel people were given red canes to assist them in walking over the lawns and gardens. But more importantly, a red cane leaned against an outhouse was the sign that a guest was occupying it at the time.

The waters at the resort were cathartic and sent the patrons rushing for the nearest outhouse at strange times. There was no need for the outhouse doors to have locks because such gracious people always respected a red cane outside the outhouse.

After years of an efficiently run resort, someone with a penchant for pranks arrived. Pandemonium broke out when guests needing to use the facilities found themselves standing in line at the outhouses for what seemed like an eternity. Finally, some brave soul knocked discreetly on a few doors only to be greeted by silence. It seems that the prankster had placed red canes outside every single outhouse as a joke. It wasn't long after that incident that door locks replaced the red cane system at the elegant French Lick resort.

'NORIE AND THE PALLBEARERS

By Gail Larson Toerpe

In the early 1950s when my parents had been married nearly 25 years, they finally had enough money to buy a small plot of land on which to build a vacation cottage. Although the land was in middle Wisconsin, we called it up north.

As soon as they signed the papers, Mom and Dad began collecting items for up north.It was as if they started their own little cottage industry. Being frugal and conservative, they bought whatever they could at rummage sales, estate sales, and second-hand shops. Each time they found some old *new* thing, they got as excited as kids at a circus. Although we were surprised by their enthusiasm, my brother, two sisters and I got a kick out of the sparks that lit up our folks' lives.

My siblings and I noted the glimmer in Dad's eyes when he found an old well pump they could use at the cottage. We giggled at Mom's delight when she discovered several low-priced ancient lanterns at an estate sale. But the best day of all was the day Mom and Dad found a timeworn outhouse for sale on a farm on the outskirts of town.

When Mom saw the outhouse she quoted from *old lonesome* George Gobel of 1950s TV fame, "You know," she said, "You just can't hardly git them no more!"

By spring of 1956 there were still no buildings standing on the property up north. In fact, there was no road leading up to no buildings. But at least now we had an outhouse to put in place.

As the six of us gathered toward the front end of the long muddy path to the acreage, we debated how to carry the

66

old two-seater. The most logical way, we decided, was horizontally, coffin fashion.

Since the popular Rodgers and Hammerstein musical, *Oklahoma,* was a top movie that year, a particular song from the film seemed appropriate for the trek. So, as the six pallbearers moved along the soggy path lugging the well-worn outhouse, all joined in to sing, "Pore Judd is daid, pore Judd Frye is daid. He's lookin' oh, sa peaceful and sa nice. He looks like he's asleep, it's a shame that he won't keep...but it's summer and we're runnin' outta ice!"

It's been many years since we carried that outhouse to its final resting place up north and although up north is no longer ours, I just hope that the antique two-seater was preserved and has found a place near the hearts and cheeks of the new owners. Hopefully, they even kept the specially painted sign that personalized our outhouse: *The 'Norie,* named after my mother, Lenore.

THE OUTHOUSE AT BOOGER HOLLOW

By Marcy Kearns

One of my favorite memories of my childhood is the classic facility at Booger Hollow, Arkansas, in the heart of the Ozarks. I don't think Booger Hollow is in the Rand McNally. But I definitely remember passing through it on the way to Eureka Springs or Branson, Missouri. As we headed south during a family vacation, all we saw of Booger Hollow was a sign, hand-painted on knotty wood, declaring "POPULATION: 8... AND A DOG." The "8" was actually crossed out and a 7 was scratched in its place. Must have been a funeral in Booger Hollow that year.

We saw one other thing in Booger Hollow that day...the most precious monument to mankind that ever came out of Ozark moonshine stories...a country outhouse. It stood off the road's shoulder, on an incline, the centerpiece of a bare patch in the woods. Dandelions and stinging broad-leafed grass edged its walls. The magnificent outhouse was painted the color of a rusty Radio Flyer red wagon. A patrol of crickets guarded the outhouse, but let us sneak by so we could do our business. Before we left I took a quick snapshot, making sure I captured the half-moon carved in its door.

That outhouse in Booger Hollow, if it's still there, is undoubtedly the most charming rest stop in the Ozarks. I'd recommend it highly if you ever feel the call while tramping through that part of the country.

WEE-WEE ANTS ON THE OUTHOUSE TRAIL

By John Reardon

When the children were younger, our family was on an exploration trip with another family in Belize in Central America. Upon arrival, we were greeted by waterfalls and pools in the most beautiful natural paradise in God's world. My wife, Josie, and I, the other couple and all our children eagerly settled down to swimming, jumping and floating in the sun warmed pools. Before long, Josie spotted a tiny building at the top of a hill. Since nature was calling, she decided to climb the hill in the hot Central American sun while the rest of us relaxed in the beautiful pools below. She climbed and climbed to the top of the long hill until she reached her destination where she quickly disappeared into the tiny building. In two seconds she reappeared and descended the hill back to the river.

Both families continued to relax as the children romped in the water. I waited for my wife to return, curious to hear her description of what she'd found up above. Josie was disgruntled, "Why, that building barely has enough boards in the walls to qualify it as a building! And it's just that, a building, not an outhouse! I can't imagine what it's used for."

We continued our trip by van across the beautiful land of Belize. When we came to another river we all got out and waded across while my friend Ken gingerly maneuvered the van across the riverbed. As we traveled along the narrow road, we passed some sugar cane fields being cleared by fire. It was a little disconcerting when we saw that the fires were totally unattended and in some places were roaring and wild. We continued along to our quarters for the night. Both of our families were invited to stay in a missionary campground located on the banks of a river near the Guatemalan border.

As we settled down for the night, the missionaries told us not to worry because the grounds were protected by armed guards. Now we all know when someone tells you not to worry, you worry. We'd heard of the political unrest in the area but, at the moment, we were more concerned with not getting in the way of the "wee-wee" ants. These are tiny creatures that happen to like a certain type of leaf. The problem was that the special leaves grew some distance away from the ants' nests. The ants had set up a highway in the field for their foraging expeditions that consisted of a two-inch wide, close-cropped, two-lane road. One lane was for the wee-wee ants who were heading to the leaf feast and one lane was for those returning. We'd been warned to choose our campsite carefully because the ant army disliked anything that happened to block their roadway and they'd been known to eat their way through any obstruction. We chose our campsites with care while there was enough light to check out the length of the grass.

The adults were treated to open-sided cabins for our night's rest, two per cabin. As dawn approached, Josie decided to seek out the facilities. As she glanced around the open sides of the cabin all she could see was smoke filling the entire area. She panicked when she recalled the cane field fires of the day before and the unrest of the locals at the border. All thoughts of using the outhouse that was located 50 yards away were forgotten.

"John, wake up! There's fire all around us!" Josie shouted.

As I woke up and my eyes cleared, I proceeded out into the smoky area. Funny thing, I couldn't smell any smoke. That's when I realized the smoke we'd worked ourselves into a panic over was nothing more than river fog that engulfed the area every morning. Josie was so relieved...in more ways than one, especially after she located the elusive outhouse still enshrouded in the morning fog of Central America.

THE RED-FACED MINISTER

By E. Joyce Schulte

Growing up in rural, Protestant Missouri, I learned early that courtesy was to be practiced every day and with every person.

Our rural church owned, among other things, one of the nicest and cleanest privies in the area. Since the church membership was growing, the new privy had been built with two holes and with steps at one of the holes just for little kids. We felt we were right uptown.

When the church was cleaned on a weekly schedule by one of the church families, the privy was also cleaned. After toilet paper came to be popular in our part of the country, the roll in the privy also was checked. Someone was sure to say, "Be sure there's enough for Sunday."

The ladies of the church frequently met during the week for various events: quilting, fellowship, dinners or to provide funeral meals. On one of those days one of the female pillars of the church excused herself from the event and made her way to the privy out behind the church. She'd been in the outhouse some few minutes when the door opened suddenly and she found herself looking directly into the face of the new-to-the-congregation minister. But training in genteel Missouri courtesy took over, and without missing too many seconds, she said, simply, "Do come in!"

The red-faced minister, too embarrassed to say anything, simply shut the door quickly and no doubt ran from the outhouse full force.

CATS, CATALOGS AND CONSTIPATION

By Dorothy Jacobs

I was eight years old in 1934 when our family moved to a different farm, east of Sterling, Illinois. After getting the milk cows settled in their new barn, Dad's next job was to clean the outhouse. It seemed that the renters before us always let the holes in the outhouse fill clear up, something my Dad didn't appreciate. So he hooked up his horses to the manure spreader. After tipping the outhouse on its side, he used the horses and the manure spreader to clean out the holes and dig them a little deeper. Then Mother got busy and scrubbed out the holes with wash water. After that, she put in a new box for the old catalog and the outhouse was ready for business. Only trouble was that the door always dragged on the bottom, so it could never quite close tight. But Dad said it was better that way because it would keep the old outhouse aired out and that's why he never fixed it.

Like most farms, ours had cats, wild ones. They were always born in the barn and were kept around and fed only because they were great mice chasers. We were never allowed to have one for a pet in the house. One day Dad stormed into the house. "That darn stray white cat had her babies in the outhouse! Four of them! Right there in the catalog box. Mama, have you got another box we can use for the catalog?"

I was surprised that Dad didn't plan to move the cats. Instead, he warned my sister and me not to touch the kittens because he said if we did they might get sore eyes. Mother added that if we touched them, the mother cat would probably move them.

Dad smiled and said, "Well, go ahead and touch them. Then at least we'll have 'em out of the outhouse."

72

Of course my sister and I wouldn't think of touching those cats because we liked visiting them every time we had to go to the outhouse to do our business. In fact, every member of our family enjoyed those kittens in the outhouse. We noticed that even the hired man and Dad spent more time out there. Daddy even named them: Fluffy, Blacky, Tabby and Calico.

Eventually, after the kittens grew to be self-sufficient, they all moved out to the barn where they could get good warm milk from the cows. About this time it was summer and the wasps moved into the outhouse. Mama told us to be sure and get in and out fast so the wasps wouldn't get us. I developed such a fast-paced bathroom habit that summer that it's still with me today. I never spend much time in a restroom, not even when I worked full time in a factory and could have taken a nice break in the rest room.

Years ago, most of us kids were constipated and I believe it was because of the outhouses. They were all cold, dark and away from the house. I believed the bogeyman stayed out there at night and since no one wanted to take us out there after dark, if we had to go, we often put it off and constipation became a way of life.

Farewell to that necessary old outhouse. It will live in my memory...but I'm sure glad they're all in the past. At least most of them are!

KNOTHOLE IN THE OUTHOUSE WALL

By Mary Rosina Baer

"Hear the birdie, Mommy?"

My three-year-old son and I heard a cardinal sing as we ambled to the outhouse on our first morning of camping at Shute Pond, Wisconsin. Michael had taken care of half his elimination needs since we arrived in the woods, as little boys tend to do when living outdoors. His dad, four siblings and I had simply looked the other way. But now it was time to attempt the big job.

We scuffed along. Each bush, each pebble, every bird call and every tree caught his attention. "Yook, Mommy," he said, "Yook at that!"

Michael's hand slipped out of my grasp as I began to hurry the project along to get to the more pleasant part of camping. He headed straight for the poison ivy. I grabbed him just in time.

In the distance the rustic structure tilted slightly. And, yes, a half-moon was carved into the door. A block away, he froze. "Mell," he balked, "What's THAT?"

"What is what?" I asked innocently, taking a firmer grip of his hand.

He wrinkled his nose. "That 'mell!" He planted his sturdy legs firmly.

A cardinal yodeled again. "Oh, see the cardinal. I pointed to the top branch of an elm tree. "Listen!"

"I wanna go back," he whined.

"See? There he goes."

Distracted, he watched and walked with me.

"We're meeting Daddy at the camp store *after* we go potty. See? There's the red sign." I pointed. "Oh look! There goes the cardinal's mate." We were almost there.

"'Mell," he stopped walking and held his nose.

"What a good idea!" I held my nose, too.

He ran. His legs pumped faster than I could react. He reached the camp store and leaped into his dad's arms.

"'Mell!" he screamed.

Our first attempt? Failure.

Two days passed before we made another trek.

Meanwhile, I discovered a strategic knothole in the side wall just about eye level for a seated three-year-old.

The following morning, Mike and I returned. He seemed to be in real distress so we walked briskly, noted the wildlife and avoided discussing our destination until opposite the outhouse.

"I have something to show you, Michael," I said quietly.

"'Mell, Mommy," he replied as we got closer.

"Yes, I know." I held my nose. "I found a special hole inside. It's a secret hole just for Mike. Come in and see."

Intrigued, he ran to the door. I scooped him up, lowered his britches, quickly sat him down on the well-worn seat and pointed to the hole at his eye level. "Look out there, honey. What do you see?"

He squinted out the hole. "Sky. Trees."

"Great. See any squirrels? Birds?"

Mike squinted while he grunted. "Hmmmm. One bird. Red!"

"Must be that cardinal we saw the other day."

Mike put his finger into the knothole and relaxed. Results happened. Mike smiled. I smiled.

"Hear the birdie, Mommy?"

For the remainder of the camping trip, we made two, four, maybe six trips per day to the outhouse so Michael could do his business, and of course to see the knothole in the wall. To this day I believe that knothole was Michael's favorite part of that entire camping trip.

BLARNEY, BEES, AND BARE BEHINDS

By Sue Burke

It was simply a fine Saturday summer morning in central Wisconsin. A bit of fog glowed pink in the sunrise and curled around the reeds at the shores of Spring Lake. Birds warbled, frogs splashed and a nearby field of alfalfa scented the air gently.

The outhouse sat on a hill next to the graveled parking area at little Spring Lake's public boat launch. A few miles away, our family kept a summer cottage on the shores of Green Lake. On long afternoons when the heat bugs buzzed or during breaks in late evening card games, my father and grandfather would entertain us and themselves by re-enacting one of their large repertoire of dubious tales. Like the time they toured in a circus. They had a high dive act – they claimed – and over successive summers, the pool of water at the foot of the diving board shrank considerably. Eventually, as Dad would pause dramatically at the edge of an imaginary diving board a hundred feet high in the circus tent, Grandpa would run an imaginary handkerchief across his forehead, wring it out, and place it on the floor. That was the target. Quite often in their story, Queen Victoria would order a command performance.

Sometimes Dad and Grandpa panned for gold in Alaska. Or California. Sometimes they fought in the Civil War, hunted whales or did whatever had been featured in a recent television show or was the topic of school lessons for me or my brothers and sister.

Other stories drew on personal events. Dad and Grandpa told about the building of the cottage, about generations of childhood mishaps or about Dad's tour in the

76

Marines, during which he bravely kept Virginia safe from the North Koreans.

And fish stories. They had a million fish stories. The ones that got away, the ones that should have gotten away and the lures that could hook anything but a live fish. Once a seagull grabbed a minnow in midair as my grandfather cast out his bait. Again and again, on the screen porch, Grandpa would re-enact the catch, reeling in the hooked bird from the sky, ducking as the seagull's mate dive-bombed him.

On one particular summer Saturday morning Dad and Grandpa got up before dawn to haul their boat to the sparkling clear waters of Spring Lake to try for a few northern pike. After a while, they returned to the public boat launch so my father could use the outhouse.

"And there I was sitting there, minding my own business," my father would say, an aggrieved tone always in his voice, "when I felt the floor vibrate under my feet. Then I felt something tickling my behind. What could be tickling me in an outhouse, I wondered?"

Dad said he looked down into the pit of the outhouse. He saw nothing. He was baffled. So he sat down again.

Suddenly he felt a sharp, stinging pain. The bee that was crawling on his behind had stung him. As he leapt to his feet, another got him. The vibration in the floor turned into a snarl. Bees lived in that outhouse floor, and they meant to guard their home from any intrusion.

With his pants and undershorts still around his knees, my father fled. Bees pursued. He hobbled down the path on the hill. Another bee got him. He pulled up his pants, more in the interest of gaining speed and protection than for modesty. Gravel crunched under his feet as he dashed across the parking lot and shouted to Grandpa. With the wisdom of accumulated years, Grandpa assessed the situation. What they needed was a fast getaway, and he was the man for the job.

In a flash, with the unerring skill of an accomplished fisherman, Grandpa untied the boat from the pier posts and revved up the old Evinrude motor. My father scrambled up the short pier, angry bees in a swarm right behind him. Grandpa carefully gauged speed and distances and, at just the right moment, shoved off from the pier.

And then —

"I know," sometimes my little brother would interrupt. He'd hop off the sofa and take Grandpa's place in the story, one hand on the tiller of the outboard and the other grabbing an imaginary cap off his head. He'd swat away the last few pursuing bees as he steered the boat out into the safety of the lake over waves of laughter.

Wild America. Dad and Grandpa warned us. There was the time they tracked the yeti in the Himalayas. Or was it Bigfoot in the Rockies? Wherever it was, Dad and Grandpa almost got him.

Over the years we learned that you never know when you might be attacked, maybe by wolves that pursued gold hunters in Alaska, or maybe by the circus lions, or maybe even by outhouse bees.

At least Mother confirmed the bees-in-the-outhouse story. She personally observed three bee stings on my father's behind. She thought it was funny. Every time Dad told the story, he fought a smile and insisted it wasn't.

"And why," he'd ask every time, still aggrieved until the day he died, "would bees want to live in an outhouse floor?"

HOW TO BUILD AN OUTHOUSE

By Bob Jansen

An outhouse is a little house behind a big one. It's usually found in a country setting where no city sewers are available. They look fairly simple, and for that reason are often built by amateurs.

You have to build at least two outhouses before you become an expert. I learned what I know from making mistakes; the first when I built one next to an apple tree on our lake property. I soon discovered there is no sound in nature as disturbing when you're sitting in an outhouse thinking or meditating as apples dropping on the roof. Besides, the ground around an apple tree does not absorb moisture very well: I could have slid off the path and ended up with a broken arm or leg. So, the location is very important.

First, dig the hole deep and wide. A small outhouse over a big hole is better than a big outhouse over a small hole. If you dig it deep and wide enough, you won't have to dig again.

Now about the construction: You can use either joists or beams. Beams cost more but will last forever. If you choose joists and a lot of heavy people use the outhouse, with time the joists will give way and the whole building will come crashing down.

You have a choice between a pitch roof or lean-to. A pitch roof is nicer to look at but a lean-to is best for many reasons. First of all, it has less corners for yellow jackets and wasps to build their nests in. There is nothing more disturbing than a big wasp buzzing around your head when you're sitting there trying to get a little rest or reading the catalog.

When planning the furnishings, remember that a lot of older folks still prefer a catalog to toilet tissue. It's more economical. J.C. Penney still puts out two pretty good ones every year, and if you discount the stiff colored sheets, you can expect to get year-round service. Not only is it useful, but it is interesting reading. With all the recycling we read about these days, catalogs are coming back in style.

I checked and found that if you put your Penney's catalog in a six-person three-holer in early spring, you will be in men's underwear before the snow flies. If you have an 80-year-old in the family, he or she might still insist on corn cobs. Young people would ask you, "What for?" Don't answer that; just put a box of cobs in the corner. It won't cost anything and someone may thank you. Old people get set in their ways.

Don't cut the holes too comfortably, and whatever you do, never put a modern toilet seat in your outhouse. Your guests will stay out there for hours at a time with the door locked. They might even fall asleep, and your outhouse will be out of service until they wake up.

If you build your outhouse too close to an expressway ramp, strangers will stop and use it. Maybe they just want to break the monotony or maybe they miss the outhouse they used during childhood. Whatever the reason, you have to be neighborly and let them use it, but I suggest you install a speaker below the seat, with a microphone in your kitchen. If they stay too long, you can hurry them by speaking into the mike in a loud, clear voice: "Would you please move over to the next hole? I'm painting down here!" In less than two minutes, you will see them fly out the door and never come back.

Halloween is the worst time of year for outhouse owners. Some people still can't resist the urge to tip one over. To avoid that, I suggest you anchor it. Take a ten-foot plank and screw it to the back of your outhouse with six feet of it in the hole. Halloween night will come and go, but you will never see your outhouse tipped over.

Of course you'll need a good latch for the door. You can choose a spool and string or a hook and eye. A spool and string costs almost nothing, but the system is not dependable. Either the spool or the string will break and you'll be caught. Use a hook and eye of the best quality, and rest secure.

I don't recommend windows. Picture yourself in there, meditating or just dozing. Someone comes to the door and finds it locked. They are sure to look in the windows, and then you don't get the privacy you came there for.

It is customary to cut a design in the door. Most folks like a crescent moon or twining hearts. Any design will give good ventilation, but be sure to cut it high enough so people can't peek in and see what you're up to.

The door should swing in, never out. If you're sitting there with the door open at about a 45-degree angle to let in the sun and air, and you hear someone coming, you can kick it shut with your foot. But if the door swings out, you can't get up off the seat to reach around to close it without getting caught. That's one thing I learned the hard way.

Face your outhouse east so you get the full benefit of the sun. You can plant rhubarb and asparagus behind the outhouse. They'll grow like crazy.

If money is no object, you can add a few amenities such as electricity for a heater in winter and an air conditioner for summer. You can install a ceiling fan and line the interior walls with Celotex insulation. You can install a roof gutter and lightning rod. A fire extinguisher can be added, as well as a telephone or maybe a small television set and stereo. You can impress your neighbors by putting your house number on the door. Use your regular house number and just add the letter A. If you are an avid reader, you may want a bookshelf.

A friend of mine suggested a two-story outhouse with a disappearing stairway. I thought the idea would be impractical because it might be hard to find a tenant for the lower unit.

GRAPES AND GRAND AUNTS ON THE PRIVY PATH

By Marion Shaw

Have you ever heard someone say in fun, "They have a path instead of a bath?" That's exactly what it was at Aunt Mattie's. The path began at the kitchen door and followed the line of grapes on the grape arbor straight out to the outhouse.

The privy door faced out onto the path, a welcome sight if you were in a hurry. This was kept fastened with a hook low enough for the short people as well as the grownups. Inside, it was about six feet square. A bench across the back had two holes cut in the seat. Some people with better accommodations had three holes. At Aunt Mattie's, one of the two holes was about twelve inches across and the other one, just eight inches across for people my size.

At Aunt Mattie's, there were other accommodations too, like lids over the holes and vents at each side near the roof so big folks could look out when they stood up or I could when I stood tiptoe on the seat. A country road was near Aunt Mattie's outhouse and no telling when you would want to know who and what was causing the noise out there.

You were instructed right off that the bucket of white powder in the corner was lime and it was to be used each time to cover anything left down below. I can still hear Aunt Mattie, "The lime keeps the flies away, you know, and that's not all, it's 'spensive so don't use more than you need."

Of course, the best part was the old Sears, Roebuck and Montgomery Ward catalogs. They sure were treasured; the new ones in the house and the old ones in the outhouse. You could get caught up on all kinds of speculation and dreaming. Big folks seemed to be interested in how the fashions and the prices were always changing. Aunt Mattie and I could sit side by side and have some real good times talking. Maybe that's what I miss when life gets to spinning so fast these days.

The catalogs had some interesting stiff colored pages, but we kept an empty can for those to be taken to the house to be burned in the stove. Those not so crisp were the ones to use in the outhouse and they were dropped below. When all important matters had been dropped, we limed properly, covered the seats and prepared to leave, closing the door and hooking it. One time I forgot to hook the door. An old hen went in and scratched herself a nest of Sears catalog paper and laid an egg. Let me tell you, that story was told many times, and every time I had a red face.

One time when Aunt Helen and I made that trip on the path and started back, she asked me if I had ever had a grape leaf dress. My eyes got big and I was sold on finding out about this new idea. I looked at the huge grape leaves along the path as Aunt Helen sat down on the bench next to the smoke house. She asked me to start picking the biggest grape leaves I could find. "Be sure to get leaves that have long stems," she said. Then she broke the stems off so she could use them for pins. She pinned those big grape leaves together all over my torso until I was covered with a grape leaf dress. The whole time Aunt Helen talked to me about when she was a girl. I'll never forget that wonderful afternoon on the privy path.

Many times the path was used for other reasons. It wasn't unusual for robins to build a nest in the grapevines. What fun it was to keep tabs on the progress of that family. My knowledge of the stars was learned on nighttime trips on the path with Aunt Mattie. She was never in a hurry and always willing to try to satisfy a little girl's curiosity.

Don't feel bad if you don't have a path in your memory bank like I do. After all, everyone's path is always a little different. Mine was just lined with grapes and grand aunts, that's all.

OUTHOUSE FIT FOR A CITY GIRL

By Marianne Wenger Severson

"What do you mean we can't use the toilet in our bathroom?"

"Not until we get our own land, dear...this mobile home is just temporary," my husband, Oral, said.

I was a city bred girl transported to the north woods with my husband, sister and brother-in-law during the hunting and fishing season.

Oral pointed out that the outhouse out back would be our bathroom in the meantime.

One problem with that imitation brick asphalt-sided privy was the fact that neither my sister, Doris, nor I could reach the holes. So the men got busy putting their carpentry skills to use. They made a step all across the floor of the outhouse. They covered the floor and step with carpeting and put newly purchased toilet seats over the holes. Doris even put curtains over the windows.

The first time I went in, I was surprised at how cozy it looked. Doris even had matches and candles in fancy candleholders sitting about.

"Doris, I've dined by candlelight, read by candlelight, but never...never...*that* by candlelight," I laughed.

One evening I went into the outhouse and before I had a chance to light a candle, I was staring into the face of a porcupine. I got out of there faster than a Green Bay Packer running back!

These days we're spoiled with our garden tubs, saunas and whirlpools. Most of us don't appreciate what our forefathers had to endure daily. The good old days weren't really that good.

But we were lucky. We had the plushest country outhouse I ever saw and nobody ever knocked it over.

MUCH ADO-DO ABOUT OUTHOUSES

By J. Paul Salois

When the radio station I owned was young, we decided to put on a country music show with mostly local talent, with the proceeds going to charity. This show, to be held in a pasture behind the radio station, was promptly dubbed *The Cow Pasture Concert* and was held each September for many years. The first year, we made no allowances for restroom facilities. As a result, the unexpectedly large crowd completely overwhelmed the bathroom in our studio building, which was actually a mobile home.

The second year, I borrowed a couple of outhouses from area farmers. The outcry, mainly from the women, was deafening. The boards were too rough; the space was too small; the door opening exposed the occupant to view; the line was too long. Our studio bathroom facilities came under siege again. Obviously, we still didn't have it right.

While preparing for the third annual *Cow Pasture Concert,* we asked for volunteers to come on a certain day to build an outhouse for the men and another for the women. We promoted the event as Big John Day. A hundred or so volunteers turned up with tools in hand. A local sawmill donated rough cut sycamore boards. We figured we had enough wood for fairly large units and we wouldn't have to worry about roofs because this was to be a fair weather event. If it rained, we just simply wouldn't have a show. The local hardware store gave us nails and we worked from early morning to dusk and completed two remarkable buildings, a two-holer with a four-foot trough urinal for the men and a ten-holer for the women. We were very proud of the women's facility as we had made a partition down the middle and installed five holes on each side of the partition with dividing panels for a certain degree of privacy. Someone had brought ten real toilet seats. A large panel blocked any view into the doorway. We were convinced that this year at last, we would be able to keep people out of our radio studio.

Concert day finally rolled around and the carpenter volunteers and I glowed in the knowledge that we had done a beautiful job. There would be no complaints from the women this year.

Of course I was quite busy with the third annual *Cow Pasture Concert*. Big city television stations sent camera crews, newspaper photographers were everywhere. Local airports organized sight-seeing flights. With about 6,000 people sitting on the ground in a cow pasture we had created a fantastic event. It was especially amazing when you consider that our city population was less than 3,000 people. Food booths were provided by Lions and Rotary clubs. Boy Scout troops directed the parking on several local farmers' fields. The state highway patrol had a dozen troopers to try to keep traffic moving. I was so proud that we had done everything right. The music blared forth and the people cheered.

Imagine my surprise when I took a break from the TV interviews and found a line of 40 or so women and children at the back door of our radio station trailer waiting to use the single bathroom inside. What, I wondered, could have gone wrong with our women's outhouse, our fabulous ten-holer? I trudged across the crowded pasture to the women's facility and only a couple of people went in or out during the time I observed it. It took a while for me to find out what the trouble was. The women complained that the lack of a roof made them nervous when airplanes or helicopters went by on photographic or sightseeing trips. They were especially disturbed by the sky divers who swooped over the building.

There is a whole lot more to know about outhouses than most people realize. I'm learning though…and someday I'll get it right.

RECYCLING ON THE FARM

By Hope Irvin Marston

When you come from a large family, you don't have too many private places where you can sit and daydream. Our outhouse was in use until I was about eight years old. I don't recall having to stand in line when nature called, probably because ours was a two-holer. Of course, if you wanted privacy, it was assured by use of a wooden bar on the inside.

Often I sat in there, looked out at the big apple tree and decided what I'd do with the rest of my life. I planned wardrobe after wardrobe from the pages of our Sears, Roebuck or "Monkey" Ward catalogs. Those plans were fulfilled only in my dreams since my mother made our clothing. The closest they came to realization was when I picked out my favorite pieces of yard goods. However, by the time the recycled catalog reached our outhouse, it had been replaced with a new one with different cloth to choose from.

One of the lessons we learned at an early age was how to choose the proper page from the catalog. The best choice was the index. Those off-white, beige or yellow pages couldn't compare with Bounty towels, but they were miles ahead of the glossy sheets. Consequently, they were used up fast. There were, after all, eleven of us plus our hired hand.

Reluctantly, we tore out the next best pages…those with black and white pictures. They didn't work so well, but they were tolerable.

The day eventually arrived when all that remained were the glossy pages. Using them was like trying to dry a very wet floor with a silk mop. It was better than nothing, but not much.

To make the pages more absorbent we grabbed the top and the bottom and wrinkled them until they were limp. It wasn't Cottonelle, but it served the purpose.

According to my dictionary, toilet tissue has been around since 1880. It didn't get to our farm in central Pennsylvania until about 60 years later. Until it did we learned to make do with what was at hand...a catalog full of hopes and dreams that was printed on paper that was definitely not absorbent enough!

THE TWO-ROOM OUTHOUSE

By Dorothy DuNard

The outhouse at the historic Maclay home in Tipton, Missouri, will live in my memory when everything else of the July 4, 1992, Ice Cream Social fades.

This 17-room mansion was built in 1858 and used three years later during the Civil War as the headquarters of General John Fremont. The heirs to the Maclay property left it to the state of Missouri, which turned it over to "The Friends of the Maclay Home, Inc." to preserve its history. The heirs also left all the furniture, pictures, china, crystal, and art pieces that had been in the home. In additional to all this finery, the fancy hollyhock-enhanced outhouse that boasts two rooms still adorns the grounds.

One room in the outhouse has two holes. The other room has three holes, including a short one for children. When the family occupied the Maclay home, some of its residents were elderly. On a winter's morning, the maid would take out a scuttle of coals to warm the outhouse for them.

On July 4, 1992, my friend, Martha Maclay Lawrence, who lives in Berkeley, California, returned to Tipton for the celebration and asked me to join her. As a direct descendant of the Maclay family, whenever she returns to Tipton she stays at the mansion in what she calls the Blue Room on the third floor. After the Ice Cream Social was over and all the visitors had left, Martha and I prepared to spend the night. I chose a bedroom on the first floor. Having recently sprained my ankle, I didn't relish climbing stairs.

It had been a typical, hot humid Missouri July 4th. We drank gallons of lemonade. Martha said I could use the outhouse, which is close to the home, in case nature called during the night. She also gave me a key to a modern facility that The Friends of the Maclay Home had built at the back of the lot. It had separate boys and girls facilities with flush toilets and a sink. However, it was quite a walk from the main house to this modern convenience.

I woke up around 2 a.m. and moaned, "Oh, the lemonade!" It was pouring rain. I put on my slippers and robe and headed for the outhouse. I opened the door. I tried to raise the seat. It was nailed down. I figured that must have been done when the new facility was built. But at this particular moment, as the rain poured on, I was desperate.

I headed for the back of the lot. Dark, oh my, was it dark! Try Tipton, Missouri, in the middle of the night when it's raining. I had no flashlight. I couldn't even see the padlocks on the doors. I had to feel around the building. Finally, I found a padlock and wondered, "Is this the boys or the girls?" I almost screamed, "Who cares!" Finally, I managed to get it unlocked. Within a minute you could have heard my sigh all over Tipton.

Like a long, tall Maclay ghost, I ran back in the rain to the house. Robe, bedroom slippers and hair sopping wet, I dropped onto the edge of the bed, weak with laughter. Here I sat in this great historic monument where a Civil War general had held court...where important Missouri natives had once lived...where priceless antiques abound in every room...where energy created made a difference in the world. And yet, the bottom line in every human being's existence is, "Where is the john and can I get there in time, especially in the pouring rain after discovering the outhouse seats are all nailed down?"

TWO LITTLE OUTHOUSE STORIES

By Doris Cousins

CHICKEN IN THE OUTHOUSE

When I was a child, I used to visit my grandparents on their farm in Canada. They had a hen who insisted on laying her eggs in the outhouse. It was warmer out there, I guess. They tried everything to make her use the hen house, but to no avail. She only used the outhouse. So my grandparents finally made chicken stew and the problem was solved. No more eggs in the outhouse!

FRESH AIR OUTHOUSE

In 1947, we visited some old friends who lived on a very poor farm in northern Saskatchewan. When my sons saw the decrepit outhouse with no roof, they decided to help out and repair it by putting on a new roof. The old farmer said, "No way! I enjoy the sunshine and I like to look at the stars when I'm meditating out there in the old outhouse at night." And so that outhouse was one of the first sun, wind, rain, snow, sleet, hail and air-conditioned outhouses ever built.

GUARDIAN OF THE OUTHOUSE

By Joyce Van Dusen

Aside from the seasons, things never seemed to change on my grandparents' farm. Well, almost never. My sisters and I spent the whole summer there the year I was six, in the early 1930s.

We arrived after dark, so I didn't meet Mickey until the next morning. He was one of several roosters whose voices announced the dawn. The actual meeting took place when I was sent to gather eggs from the henhouse. I was greeted at the door by a husky young rooster who denied me admission. When I didn't leave immediately, he stalked forward and gave me a peck on the knee. As I turned to flee, he gave me another one on the heel. He then spread his wings and pursued me a couple hundred feet back to Grandmother's kitchen door. Mickey stopped fifteen feet away, flew to the slanting door of the root cellar and crowed his triumph over the intruder.

There were no electric lights on the farm in those days. Bedtime came shortly after supper and the evening chores were done. We usually played a game of 500 Rummy or Old Maid before we had to go to bed. The last event of the day was a trip to the outhouse.

During the day, I seemed to encounter Mickey in all of my favorite spots, and shamefully retreated from him under attack. I hadn't learned my lesson when I blithely skipped down two steps to the path leading to the outhouse, gently swinging my lantern. I believe Mickey had been lying in wait. My feet no sooner hit the dirt of the path than I heard a rush of sturdy feet and flapping wings. With horror, my head swiveled and I saw my nemesis gaining on me. I went into fright-spurred gear and slammed the door of the outhouse just in time to hear Mickey's body strike it full force.

Even though I was terrified that Mickey would be waiting for me on the outside, at least for the time being I was safe inside the outhouse, had my lantern, and for utilitarian use there was the old Sears, Roebuck catalog. I settled down to enjoy reading the catalog until the next family member demanded entrance. After hearing my tearful tale, I was escorted back to the kitchen. Mickey must have gone to bed early that night.

Could this trauma at age six account for my present-day penchant for reading anything handy when I enter the powder room, or for my quick backward glance as I descend outside steps? I have a sneaking suspicion that it does.

GOIN' DOWN FOR A DIME

By Ted Young

When I was a boy, my father, Doctor Theodore E. Young, told me this story. It seems that one time during his younger years in Kansas, he was engaged in the usual business in a double-seater outhouse. Another fellow came in, and as that gentleman was unzipping his fly, a dime fell out of his pocket and flew into the abyss below. The man promptly took out his wallet and keys and threw them into the hole.

Dad was shocked. "Why did you do that?"

The gentleman pursed his lips and said quite seriously, "You don't think I'm going down there for a dime, do ya?"

THE SEA-GOING OUTHOUSE

By Alan Van Dusen

We shipped out of Brisbane, Australia, in 1943 on a cargo ship that had been converted into a makeshift cargo troop carrier for a voyage to Port Moresby, New Guinea, during World War II. The trip was between the Great Barrier Reef and the coast of Australia in an area not likely to harbor Japanese submarines. It took about five or six days total, including a stop en route at Townsville, Australia.

Our group numbered at least 100 men. Our home was located in an upper hold of the ship where temporary bunks had been installed in high tiers of about six or eight, supported by pipe frames. There wasn't enough room between bunks to raise your knees while lying on your back.

The solitary latrine facility for our use was a temporary wooden shack, an outhouse of sorts, that had been built on the deck. It was a small lean-to type building positioned adjacent to the ship's rail, and equipped with a wooden trough that extended through one end of the shed and projected over the side of the ship. A fire hose was attached to the start of the trough, and was supplied with water from a nearby hydrant. This provided a continuous stream of water through the length of the trough and then overboard. That portion of the trough within the shack constituted our toilet. It could serve about six men at a time. Privacy was not a problem. This was the army and there were no women about.

It would be about two years yet until the war ended, and during our occupation of various tropical islands our typical latrine facilities were smelly outhouses. They were small wood sheds erected over a hole in the ground. The memory of those island outhouses makes that shipboard outhouse a very pleasant place by comparison.

ALL HALLOW EVE

By Betty Nordengren

"Pass me another Peerless, Hiram," George said.

"Me too," said Leo as he peered over the hill toward Charlie's place.

"I wonder what Charlie has planned for us tonight?"

Guffaws and snorts filled the air as the four friends leaned back against the big boulders that lined the crest of Jimmy's hillside field.

"Remember the year he was sitting in the old privy with a shotgun, waiting for us?"

"Yippee, lucky for us he'd put it down to do his business just as we laid the old outhouse on its side."

"Remember the year he was up in that old oak tree and lost his balance and was hanging by one leg?"

"Lucky for him we were there to take him to the hospital to get his leg set."

"Yeah, right after we tipped old Bertha belly up."

"We had to slop his hogs for three weeks till his leg healed."

"It was worth it."

Uproarious laughter and shouts filled the autumn dusk and set the dogs barking.

"He's getting more creative with his guard duty. Remember last year he bought all the flashlight batteries at Albert's General Store? Had the whole clan patrolling all night!"

"That was a close one all right. We had to stay up all night and ease it over at the crack of dawn."

"How about the time Little Willie was visiting his Uncle Charlie and had a late night call of nature?"

"Yah, that extra 350 pounds slowed us up some."

"Good thing, too. Just as it started to tilt he howled. Seems he had his knees jammed up against the door and couldn't move."

"We had to set it back up!"

"Lucky for him we were there to get him out."

"He was a bit shaky but got into the spirit of things and helped push the old outhouse over."

"Course he had to help Charlie rebuild it the next day."

The hilltop rocked with a round of mirth that had them rolling in the stubble.

"Tell you what. Let's go early tonight, just after dark, he'll never suspect that."

"Sure is quiet over there."

"Looks like he gave the old privy a paint job. It stands out like a beacon."

"Not for long. Let's go. By the time we get across the field it'll be dark."

"It seems farther away."

"Nah, your eyesight never was too good."

"Keep the noise down and stay low."

"Straight ahead now, one big puuuuuuu...."

An explosion of expletives hit the air as the four friends splashed, splat, squished and plunked through the mire of deep outhouse muck.

"I'm up to !!*@!!** elbows! Get me the !!!#@*&* out of here!" Leo yelped.

"Get yourself out! That ##!@*&*!! Charlie must have washed down the sides and moved the dang thing forward! Give me a hand, somebody!" Hiram brayed.

"Get your face out of that hole, Jimmy, and roll me the !@#*&! out of here," George said, pawing at the slippery grass.

"Careful, it's slippery! Stop you #@%&*! idiot, you're pulling me in," Jimmy sputtered.

"Where's the well?"

"Never mind that, here come the dogs!"

"Next year, Charlie! Next year!!"

THE GOOD OLD DAYS?
NO WAY!

By Mary King

When I was a child, we lived on a farm in Lee County in northern Illinois and did not get electricity or indoor plumbing until 1945. Our outhouse was a two-seater. The previous season's Sears, Roebuck catalog was always in the center for reading and wiping purposes. In the summer, there were spiders, flies, bees and extreme heat to contend with out there. In the winter, the icy blasts of cold air made each visit an unpleasant one. Sometimes, snow would blow inside making the door difficult to open and close. Standard equipment needed to make the trip to the outhouse at night was a trusty lantern.

I remember our old rickety, run-down outhouse with the hole in the roof. I still have a black and white photo of my eighteen-year-old brother standing on a ladder putting the finishing touches on our brand new outhouse which was built just a few feet from the old one. Before the mid-1900s, outhouses were standard equipment on all farms in our part of the country. We never thought much about it...it was just the way it was. But whenever I hear someone refer to those times as the good old days, it makes me wonder? Good old days? I don't think so. Personally, I like my comfortable, convenient indoor bathroom.

HONEYMOON IN THE OUTHOUSE

By Patricia Lorenz

I don't remember much about my first wedding. Neither my fiancee nor I were big on lavish weddings. We'd both just moved from the college where we'd graduated in southern Illinois to Denver, Colorado, and were hard at work at our first real, better-than-minimum-wage jobs. Neither of us had vacation time coming. Neither of us had any relatives in the state of Colorado. And we certainly didn't have the money to plan for a big wedding. So one day we said, "Let's do it." And we did. There were thirteen of us in the tiny chapel and later we all went out to our favorite hangout and drank margaritas and ate popcorn to celebrate our nuptials. When I look back on it, I think the wedding and the reception thereafter may have had something to do with the state of the honeymoon.

Ah, yes, the honeymoon. We both managed to get Monday off, and since the wedding was on Friday night that gave us three days. The groom, being a geologist who loved rocks and strange, natural formations and earthly occurrences, announced Saturday morning that we were going to drive to Yellowstone National Park, over 400 miles away! That man loved to drive, but I wasn't too sure about spending the bulk of my three-day honeymoon cooped up in a car. But this was back in the 1960s when men still got their own way about most everything.

So we drove. And drove. We'd jump out of the car, eat a fast meal and get right back in the car. I oohed and aahed at the incredible scenery that whizzed by at 75 miles per hour. When we reached snow drifts that were eight feet tall in northern Wyoming, he did pause for five minutes to take my picture next to them. I stood there in my sleeveless blouse and summer-weight slacks in early June and made a snowball to throw at my groom.

Back in the car we drove for hours, winding our way through mountainous roads toward Yellowstone. We arrived at dark and spent the night in a primitive, cold cabin. By noon Sunday, after a huge brunch loaded with mountain man eggs, sausage and pancakes the size of plates, I began to feel awful. I thought back to the week before the wedding and realized that I'd been constipated for an entire week. The excitement of the wedding, worrying about taking a day off work for the honeymoon, irregular meals and spending eleven hours in the car the day before, had blocked me up completely.

As I sat on a long wooden bench with a couple dozen other *Old Faithful* watchers, waiting for the 3 p.m. spectacle, I felt as if I was carrying the weight of the world in my gut. Misery was my middle name as I watched my new husband pacing back and forth, waiting for his geological wonder to blow.

This is my honeymoon, for heaven's sake! I can't let this go on! I thought.

I swallowed my shyness and gathered my courage. "Honey, I need some prune juice. Would you mind going in to the camp store and see if they have any?"

My groom, who wasn't too crazy about the possibility of missing the start of *Old Faithful's* show, dashed into the store and returned in record time, handing me a quart of room temperature prune juice.

As we sat there waiting for the explosion of one of the world's greatest natural phenomena, I drank my juice. We waited and I drank. Suddenly the geyser put on her show, spewing hot steam hundreds of feet into the air. I watched and drank my prune juice, wishing my innards could spew like that geyser.

After the show we climbed back into the car for a driving tour of the huge national park. When a bear cub ambled across the road and climbed up to the window of the car in front of us, I snapped a quick photo, finished off my quart of prune juice and wished I was back home in a nice tub of hot water, easing my intestinal pains.

As we neared the park exit later that afternoon after a long, long drive through Yellowstone's immensity, Mother Nature and the prune juice grabbed hold of my stopped-up digestive system and started the rumblings of a geyser in my gut that felt as if it would rival that of Old Faithful.

"Bob! You have to find a bathroom! I have to go! Now! Please, get to a bathroom! Hurry!"

My groom drove a half-a-mile and slammed on the brakes. "It's up there." He pointed to a thick, dense forested area.

"Up where?" I started to panic. I didn't see anything but a huge hill and thousands of trees.

"Right there, off to the right. See that building? It's an outhouse."

I shot my husband a look that would have caused flowers to wilt and slammed the car door as I bolted out. I stumbled up the steep hill and dashed toward the outhouse, noting that it was much darker up there in the forest.

"There better be lights in this place," I mumbled to myself.

It was a two-seater outhouse. No lights. No toilet paper. No nothing, expect two smelly holes and spider webs all over the place. But at that moment as Mother Nature's grip on my intestines catapulted my mind back to reality, I plopped my quickly exposed bare fanny on hole number one. One explosion after another punctuated the silence in the woods as I prayed that my new husband had the car windows rolled up and couldn't hear what I was up to up there in the woodland privy. I sat there in that smelly pit, terrorized that a bear or a snake would amble in while I was going about my business.

An hour later, after having lost approximately ten pounds, I staggered out the door, holding my slacks in front of me. "Bob!" I hollered weakly, "Could you bring some tissues up here?" At that moment I could have killed for a roll of toilet paper.

All he could find were a couple of paper napkins from the last fast-food restaurant we'd visited. I used every square inch of those napkins and then prayed that we'd get to our hotel quickly.

That night, the prune juice continued its onslaught, having realized it had to do a week's worth of work in just a day, I suppose. At any rate, at the hotel that night I quickly made my dash for the bathroom. My husband plopped down on the bed after adjusting the TV set that was hooked to the wall up near the ceiling. After an hour of percussion noises that radiated from the bathroom, he peeked in the door and said, "Honey, I know you don't feel too good, but how would it be if I adjust this TV so you can see it from in here? If you leave the door open, you can watch from in here and I can watch it from the bed. At least you won't be so lonely."

Embarrassment, disgust and misery punctuated the rest of my evening and well into the night as I sat there on the Motel 6 toilet, watching TV, as my husband spent the night alone in the bed on the other side of the bathroom wall. *Welcome to the real world of marriage*, I thought to myself as my embarrassment began to dissipate as the sounds and smells radiating from my body began to cool down. After that, all I could think about as I carefully fondled the huge, soft roll of toilet paper before me, was the horrific outhouse experience earlier that day. I'm here to tell you that I actually said prayers of thanksgiving to the Almighty for that little bit of paradise…that nice, shiny white bathroom where I spent the third night of my honeymoon.

I never did ask my husband what he thought of our first long weekend together after our wedding, but after seven years together we parted ways. I've often wondered if our strained beginning had anything to do with the demise of the marriage. Naw. It couldn't have. Could it?

LATE SEATING WAS BEST

By Bee Neeley Kuckelman

During our trip to Greece, we enjoyed viewing the ancient ruins. The tourists in our group laughed at the guide's delightful story of the public toilets, near which we were standing in the marketplace.

This public facility was a six-holer. No privacy was apparent.

Our pleasant Grecian guide told us that the high officials of long ago, not wanting to sit on the cold stone toilet seats, used to send their servants to sit on them for awhile to warm them.

My husband whispered to me that he wished he had thought of that when he was growing up on a farm in Kansas. He said he would have sent his younger brother first in the frosty winter months to warm the wooden seat in the drafty outhouse those early mornings before chores.

TOILETS: A REAL TRIP

By LeNore Stumpf

In 1970, while living in a suburb of Tokyo, I enrolled in Japanese language classes. My teacher knew that the culture of his country was as necessary for us to understand as the language so he guided his students and answered questions readily.

One early question was about unisex toilets, still common in Japan. How were we, prim and proper military wives that we were, expected to share a toilet facility with men? Did people REALLY do that? It sounded like the quintessential culture shock to us.

My teacher responded, "It's always been done in Japan and people think nothing of it." Well, I didn't think much of it either! He continued, "Just pretend you're invisible because, to the others, you are."

One day while on a tour it became necessary for me to test his theory. I was glad to see that there were stalls, without doors, in the back part of the public toilet. The problem was I had to walk between two rows of urinals to reach them. I mustered my courage and tried to pretend I was invisible and that the male occupants were, too. Desperation turned out to be a stronger motivator than propriety.

As I worked my way to the back, my childhood flashed before my eyes. I grew up sharing the three-holer on our Kansas farm, but only with those of the same gender. And yet, there were some parallels. Occasionally, for middle-of-the-night trips to the outhouse, I hadn't awakened a sister to accompany me. Sometimes I toughed it out by going alone and pretending I was invisible to any cattle rustlers or tramps who might be lurking about.

Looking back, I guess those Japanese facilities weren't too bad. At least I didn't have to brush snow off the seat. The same cannot be said, however, about the privy back on the farm.

CATASTROPHE AT KATOWICE

By Heidi Hess Saxton

The summer before my senior year at college I spent trekking across Eastern Europe as the conductor of an international goodwill music tour. There were 27 of us altogether: thirteen and a half Polish volunteers (one of the violinists was five months pregnant), thirteen Americans, and a Hungarian bus driver, Haine.

We were a motley bunch. The Poles spoke no English (except our interpreter, who was the husband of the pregnant violinist), and the Americans spoke no Polish. The bus driver spoke neither English nor Polish. The only language we had in common was German and I was the only American who spoke that, but I wasn't exactly fluent. You might say I was slicker than a pig on ice with a dictionary. The first week I spent a good deal of time practicing the words "sit down and be quiet" (in both languages) and explaining to silly young American coeds why their spandex leotards were drawing such attention as they did their morning aerobics in the hotel lobby. We learned our music, packed our bags and boarded our bus to spread beautiful music and cheer across the Polish countryside.

Two weeks later, I was ready to turn in my baton. The concerts were fun, but all the traveling, practicing and communicating (with limited success) with non-English speakers were utterly exhausting. All I wanted was a cold glass of water (we'd had nothing but tea for fear of parasites), a hot bath and a home-cooked meal.

The night we reached the charming village of Katowice, nestled in the rolling hills of southern Poland, I thought I'd lucked out. After the concert, five of us were invited to stay in a local farmhouse owned by one of the families who had organized the concert. Happily, I dragged my suitcase to a waiting car, with visions of feather beds dancing in my head.

By the time we arrived at the farmhouse, it was already growing dark. Two of the others asked to wash up and were shown to the bathroom. The first girl went in, then came back out with a strange expression on her face.

"Everything OK?" I asked her.

"Well, there was a sink and bathtub, but no toilet."

We asked our hostess if the toilet was in another part of the house. "Ah! You want the toilet. Come with me." We trooped outside and around to the back of the house. My nose told me what was coming next. The lady of the house pointed for the benefit of the rest of us. "Over there. Watch your step!"

She wasn't kidding. A small, ramshackle privy was set up beside the garden. Inside, the stench made our eyes water. And I must say Polish mosquitoes are the most indelicate and nocturnal of creatures. It was pitch dark, so we had to do the best we could, groping for the seat and swatting away the bugs at the same time.

Squat. Slap. Slap. Under my breath I cursed the idiot who created pantyhose, which provided no protection and slowed the process considerably.

Later that night, the five of us bundled into one big feather bed, and somehow I managed to get the place by the wall. In some respects that was a good thing, as I didn't have to worry about falling out. Then I realized that I had to go again.

Oh, no. Please. Not the bug house.

I turned and whispered to the girl next to me, "I gotta GO!"

"Me, too."

"But we don't have a flashlight!"

"I know." We laid there in silence for a minute, assessing the situation.

"Well..." I said hesitantly, "we could just go outside and go by moonlight."

More silence. Clearly this was not the preferred option.

"Or. . ." I made an executive decision. "Come on, let's go." *Desperate times call for desperate measures.* "The drain hole in the tub!" Quietly the two of us tiptoed out of the bedroom, in through the kitchen, and into the bathroom.

"Go ahead. I'll keep watch," I told my partner in crime. Just then I heard footsteps.

"Hello, dear," said the lady of the house. It was nearly two o'clock in the morning, but she didn't seem at all surprised to see me standing there. "You like I make you nice cup of tea?"

"Uh ... no thank you." The last thing I needed at that moment was more tea, but I thought it impolite to say so. "We forgot to ... brush our teeth."

Inside the bathroom came the sound of running water. From the tub.

"Your friend brushes teeth in tub?"

I shrugged. The door opened and my friend emerged with a decidedly lighter spring in her step. She grinned. "Ah...you can sleep so much better with...fresh breath!"

For a moment I stood there, debating what to do next. But I knew there was no way I could go through with my evil scheme now. I sighed and headed back to the bedroom. It was going to be a very long night.

SEGHE'S OPEN-AIR OUTHOUSE

By Edward J. Kobbeman

As a P-39 fighter pilot in the South Pacific during World War II, July 25, 1943, is a day I'll never forget. That day my plane was hit by a Japanese Zero as seven other P-39s and I flew from Guadalcanal in the Solomon Islands to try to intercept a flight of Japanese Zero fighters from Rabaul.

As I dove for an enemy plane in front and below me, I was hit from above and to the left. One direct hit in my tail section knocked off half the rudder and half the elevator. One shell hit the left wing, another hit the gas bay nearest the fuselage. Shrapnel hit me as it entered the cockpit, also cutting my oxygen tube. Three shells exploded inside the wing and blew a hole two feet in diameter in the bottom of that wing. One shell hit the left door of the cockpit and shot out the radio.

Knowing I'd never make it back to the base at Guadalcanal, I limped down onto the emergency landing strip at Seghe on New Georgia Island in the Solomons. That Seghe airfield had been built by U.S. Seabees in ten-and-a-half days, which gives you an idea of its primitive conditions. Most fighter plane landing strips in the South Pacific during the war were 4,000-5,000 feet long. This one was 2,800 feet long with water at both ends. Quite a few pilots ended up in the bay when trying to land there during wartime. In fact, there's still a P-38 lightning fighter plane in about twenty feet of water just off the end of that runway.

My visit to that tiny airfield included a hike to the Seghe outhouse, which was an *out*house in the best sense of the word. It was located at least twenty yards out at the end of a rickety wooden dock built straight out over a shallow bay. At the end of the dock there was a wooden seat, two feet tall. No walls, no roof. Just the solitary seat at the end of the dock with a hole in the top where the user would drop his cargo directly into the water below. That day in July in 1943, after being shot up and after using the end-of-the-dock outhouse, I hitched a ride on a C-47 transport plane back to Guadalcanal.

I landed at Seghe a couple other times that year due to inclement weather conditions and each time visited the Seghe outhouse. Before nightfall, making a trip down the long dock to the open-air, out-to-sea privy was no problem. I do remember, however, being a bit nervous after dark about my personal safety, since we had no idea how many Japanese stragglers had retreated into the interior jungle of that small island. I never saw any enemy soldiers, however, at least not on that island.

I have to admit that the open-air, end-of-the-dock outhouse didn't hold a candle to the experience of having my plane shot almost to smithereens by a Japanese Zero on that July day in 1943, but it did make for one of many interesting memories of my three tours of duty and seventeen months spent in the South Pacific during the war.

CARBIDE CAPERS

By George Peck

Growing up in the country in Southern Illinois was a real blast, especially in the early 1940s. I only knew of one family lucky enough to have indoor plumbing during those years.

The outhouses sat there, so tempting to us boys, and so toilet tipping gave us a little excitement at night. Much of the time we had to help our neighbors right them the next day, but of course we played dumb, proclaiming that we had no idea who would dare do such a dastardly deed.

There were about ten of us boys who roamed our neighborhood ranging in age from eleven to sixteen. Our fathers were coal miners so we all had carbide and carbide lamps for our night fishing trips. Most people are not familiar with carbide. It can be a very dangerous substance if not used with caution. Carbide is a compound of pea-sized gray rocks and when a small amount of water is put on the carbide, an ignitable gas is formed. If carbide is placed in a sealable container and a few drops of water is added and then the container is sealed, gas will continue to form and expand until the container explodes with a loud bang. We used carbide for our July 4th celebrations because fire crackers were not available during World War II.

Two of my boyhood chums, Ed and Bob Murray, lived on what is known as the Orient Road near West Frankfort, Illinois. Their family had an A-1, first-class, state-of-the-art Works Progress Administration outhouse built during the depression. In our neighborhood these better-than-average outhouses were rare.

Outhouses were usually located a little distance from the house, but not far from other outbuildings. Rat killing is also another form of entertainment for country boys as rats and rat holes are plentiful around the outbuildings. My fifteen-year-old friend Ed and his eleven-year-old brother Bob saw a big rat run into a rat hole close to their outhouse. A brilliant idea came to Ed, so he grabbed a big handful of carbide and poured it in the hole while Bob ran to the well to get some water. They waited a couple of minutes after pouring a little bit of water in on top of the carbide so the gas could form. Then they lit a four-foot-long cattail torch and stuck it in the rat hole. It responded with a giant KA-BOOOOM! as a flame shot from the hole. The boys were totally unprepared for the shock that followed as the door flew open and their mother ran out screaming. Needless to say, they were not in their mother's good graces for a long time.

MOONLIGHTING

By Virginia Buening Black

During the 1980s, my husband and I and another couple purchased a modest log cabin in northern Wisconsin. It was to be our woodland retreat.

I objected to tearing down the outhouse - barely visible behind the dead branches and miscellaneous cottage debris. I would clean it up so we could use it as a backup to modern-day plumbing. The fellas had no opinion. My friend and female co-owner vowed she would have nothing to do with it, not then nor after its transformation. Her childhood recollections differed from mine. In her eyes, to have to use an outhouse was a punishment. She recalled the not-so-Charmin-like quality of the Sears catalog of her youth and the admonishments of her grandfather when she complained. She was positive the smell would get her if the critters didn't. She thought it was crazy to preserve this odoriferous blemish on the legacy of farm life in the '50s. I thought the outhouse was a unique contribution to the north woods.

Actually, because I was raised in the city my exposure to outhouses was limited to the occasional visit to the country where my father's extended family lived. Their outhouse was used as a conservation measure to save the indoor plumbing during family reunions. Spiders and flies were part of the ambiance. Catalogs were something to look at in the privacy of that little house. A roll of toilet paper could always be found in a covered coffee can - perhaps as an apology for requesting the city folk to use the primitive outdoor facility.

Our outhouse in the north woods had a paneled door with cracks. Located behind years of accumulated cabin collectibles, it was a spider-infested two-seater. Inside, there was a coffee can, an etched mirror and loads of history. I had visions for this house that no one else could imagine.

After clearing it and sweeping it out, I scrubbed it down. I painted the outside a chocolate brown and the inside a creamy white. On those rough walls I found the perfect canvas for my not-so-artistic abilities and felt like a pioneer as I created a tribute to the independent woman.

Outside, I painted a blue crescent moon on the door. It had to be tipped at just the proper angle to be reminiscent of the *outhouse* style of years gone by. Eventually it slanted slightly upward with the words "Blue Moon" just above its inside curve, right where the man in the moon is supposed to sit.

Inside, I painted the floor a soft, serene Atlantic blue, the same blue as was on the door. Tiny white peaks and gentle waves continued up from the floor to the water line. I was seeking peace and tranquility.

One seat was HERS and one was HIS. Inside the lid on HERS was a blond-haired mermaid named Mattie. HIS sported a fish with spiked hair and sunglasses. The foggy etched mirror remained on the wall opposite HERS. It was during a test run that I looked back at my reflection, a reflection of what I had become. Not the me I longed to be. The key to my happiness was hidden behind that mirror and I knew this should have been a one-seater outhouse.

That old outhouse survived. The marriage didn't. In the 1990s the outhouse was once again a storage shed for things that had no place. I have a house of my own now, a Cape Cod with pine paneling. It also has paneled doors with cracks and shutters complete with crescent moons angled slightly upward to catch the good that's raining down on me and all who live here.

Both the old outhouse and my Cape Cod will be here long after I have left. I hope that my tributes to independent women from every generation in the form of creativity, ingenuity and the ability survive are also here long after I'm gone. Perhaps my epitaph will read, "Like an outhouse she survived." Like Charmin, I prefer, "Remember me softly."

FROM PATH TO BATH

By Marion Shaw

Responding to progress of the time and a growing family, my grandfather built a new home in 1885. After many years of using an outhouse down the path in back of the house, he and his family were excited about the new indoor bathroom.

His children were growing up and none of them ever grew tired of relating the story of the snippy old neighbor lady who was so shocked when she heard they were putting a complete bathroom into the new house. Quite a room it was, too, fourteen by sixteen feet, with two full size windows. It had plaster that was marked to look like tile from the floor up to the lavatory back. That lavatory was a gem. It was large enough, we learned, so that two of us could sit one on each side and wash our feet at the same time. This was, of course, when no grownups were in sight. The bath tub was long enough for even a small adult to lie down in. So when the coast was clear, we could slide down the incline if both surfaces were wet. If they were not, it became a learning experience. A moping session always followed the fun, usually before others learned of our adventures.

Most of those good farm people were surprised to see the lavatory was on a 'pee-des-til.' The young ones in the family had trouble keeping a straight face when it was said that way. But we certainly enjoyed the convenience of having running water in that indoor bathroom.

Everyone in town knew that the old neighbor lady was horrified over the bathroom in my grandfather's house, but she never did say anything to us directly. But to all who knew our family she would say in a hushed voice, "Do you know them Terrells have put a bathroom in that big house? I just never would have thought they would be the kind to do their business in their own house like that! Imagine!"

THE TRAVELING OUTHOUSE

By Alice Flower

I was peeling potatoes at the kitchen sink, beginning preparations for my supper time brood. Sensing something was not quite right, I glanced out the window, noticing a high traffic volume on our residential street. Cars were creeping by in front of the house. Some were stopped. Passengers were staring, pointing at the far side of the yard out of my window view. Curiosity compelled me to open the front door and go out onto the porch. There in my front yard reposed a large ancient outhouse. It was the week before Halloween.

Like his father, my husband is a jeweler in our small town; and like his father, he had told me of some of his juvenile pranks with outhouses around Halloween. My mind searched for the culprit. Maybe this was a latent revenge. I walked around the weathered structure to discover that it was a roomy two-holer with a sign over the door. "HAVE YOUR LOCAL FAMILY JEWELER CHECK YOUR SETTINGS."

Instead of being outraged, I doubled over laughing. I knew who was responsible...two very dear friends with whom we had exchanged harmless but extremely original *gotchas* from time to time whenever the mood came upon us. He was a car dealer.

My husband drove up at that moment and stared dumbstruck at the sight. He also knew immediately who the perpetrator was and began to mumble, grunt and laugh at the same time. "That son of a gun, I'll fix his wagon!" And so began another vendetta.

Our three boys were thrilled to have such a possession at their disposal for trick or treat season and wouldn't let us do anything with it until after the great pumpkin night. They made elaborate preparations for the occasion. A scary "body" was hung inside the privy. A ghost was fitted on the roof. Jack-o-lanterns with garish faces, lighted from within via flashlights, were placed on the inside seat and outside the door on either side. What the boys considered their greatest inspiration was putting grocery bags filled with treats into the holes. This genuinely repulsed the accompanying parents; but the little costumed beggars remained unfazed. Our inventive sons deemed the project a huge success.

Finally the time came to rid our yard of this anachronism and vindicate ourselves from the original affront. Our next-door neighbor had a pickup truck. He was hornswoggled into abetting the revenge. Chuckling and getting their hands full of splinters, our good sport neighbor, my husband and our sons loaded the outhouse onto the truck bed, albeit slightly askew. It was a quiet Sunday afternoon. The conspirators drove carefully down Main Street, virtually stopping traffic. Sunday drivers were incredulous at the extraordinary sight before them. The target was the used car lot, owned by our friend, the Buick dealer in the heart of downtown. Great effort was exerted to get the outhouse perfectly situated on the lot, facing the street to access as many onlookers as possible. The boys lettered the large sign. "WOULDN'T YOU REALLY RATHER HAVE A BUICK? BUCKET SEATS OPTIONAL."

The town was abuzz with these odd goings-on, but nothing was heard from our friends, the originators, for some time.

The convenient availability of outhouses at that time coincided with the construction of Milford Lake Reservoir. Farmers, residents and businesses of the former township of Milford, Kansas, moved quickly to higher ground as the new lake filled, taking everything of value that was portable. Folks from all around were invited to come and help themselves to anything that remained. Many salvaged bricks, limestone building rocks, porch columns and all else that appeared usable. Naturally, we learned later, our kooky friends had desperately wanted, and had helped themselves to, the old outhouse for their nefarious scheme.

All was quiet on the home front for several weeks, but one day I drove into the driveway and was greeted by a familiar sight. The bad penny potty had turned up again, listing badly, probably because its antiquity didn't lend itself to such frequent travel. This time the sign read, "JEWELS ARE LIKE HEIRLOOMS. EACH GENERATION GETS THE POT."

That night, after getting all the splinters out of his hands from the last episode, my beloved grabbed the phone and called a friend who owned a moving business. When the friend answered, my husband queried without preamble, "Do you move outhouses?"

"Absolutely!" answered the friend, not missing a beat. He'd been around for several of our prior capers and was unflappable. My husband gave some brief instructions and hung up.

Early the next morning, a huge moving van drove up and the now pathetic outhouse was placed inside. The van proceeded to the car dealer's house and the object in question was unloaded posthaste onto his front lawn. He ran outside to confront the moving men and was handed a huge bill for delivery services. Of course the car dealer had no idea it was a fake bill, and as the movers drove away, our dear friend gaped and ranted in frustration.

It is my understanding that the outhouse collapsed and "died" in the man's front yard that very same day, having served its strange purpose valiantly. It became a pile of aged boards, rusty nails and splinters, unable to withstand having had so many adventurous tours, much more exciting than anything in its previous life. Our friends confessed that they eventually hauled it to the dump. I was crestfallen. The thing had become like one of the family. The least they could have done was use it for kindling and obtained an urn for the ashes.

THE HONEY WAGON DISASTER

By Joseph A. Visintainer

In the mid-1930s when I was president of the village of Caspian, Michigan, in the Upper Peninsula, I recall an incident that happened one night that had the town talking for months. During those Depression years, there were still 150-200 outhouses in town, all built in a similar fashion by a local carpenter. The outhouses were made with several timbers on the ground and the outhouses could be lifted off the timbers so that work could be done below or so that the pits below could be cleaned out periodically.

During those years it was too costly to dig new holes and move the outhouses when they filled up, so two men were hired to shovel the waste out by hand. They were paid an excellent salary of $5 per outhouse. Both men were heavy liquor drinkers and didn't seem to have much of a sense of smell. One man would go down into the hole wearing hip boots. He shoveled waste into a pail. The second man pulled the pail up to the surface with a rope and dumped it into the horse-driven wagon called the honey wagon.

One night when the honey wagon was full and peacefully riding through town to be emptied at the waste site, Felix, the town daredevil, appeared. He had the only motorcycle in town and came racing by the horse-driven honey wagon. The horses were terrified! They reared up, tipped the wagon over and dumped all the waste on the road right in front of the town hall. The fire department was called out and those poor firemen had to spend the rest of the night using their powerful hoses to wash the mess into the nearby Iron River.

BOO

By Lola Jones

It was 1937, early fall, on a farm in central Wisconsin. I was a very brave eight year old. Even though it was dark out I could go out to the outhouse all my myself.

Supper was ready but nature had called, so I took my light and set out for the *little house.* On my way out there I noticed a light going back and forth in the field and I knew my father was on his way to the house after milking and bedding down the cattle for the night.

I slipped in the door and latched it. By the light of my kerosene lantern I skimmed the funnies. They were about a month old, but *The Katzenjammer Kids* and *Andy Gump* always made me laugh. Since I had read them many times, I decided to do my business and get out of there.

As I started to open the door, a voice exploded with the word, "Boo!"

I slammed the door shut, braced my back against the seat and with legs outstretched, planted my feet firmly against the door. My heart was pounding and my legs felt shaky, but I locked them to make sure nothing came after me through that door.

As I sat breathlessly on the floor, the apologetic voice of my father came from the other side of the door saying, "It's only me."

Speechless, I pondered if some spook could imitate my father's voice. Maybe something was with him forcing him to coax his little girl out.

"It's all right, Lola honey," Daddy continued. "I was just trying to be funny. Please come on out and I'll walk you to the house. I'm sorry I scared you."

I was scarcely breathing. Maybe it would be better to wait until whoever was there left and then I could run for the house.

"Won't you please come out for your old Dad, honey? I promise I won't play any more tricks on you," Daddy cajoled.

Maybe it really was Daddy. I could, at least, peek out and see. I tried to bend my legs, but they stayed straight and the door remained shut tight. I could hear something or someone working the latch. It must be Daddy, I told myself, but I couldn't speak and my legs would not bend.

It seemed like I was there for hours and pretty soon I heard my mother's voice. "There's nothing bad out here, Lola," she promised. "Come on out and have supper with us."

"I'm sorry, Lola, so sorry," Dad pleaded. "Please come out. I'll never do it again." Daddy begged and Mom coaxed and I cowered inside the outhouse.

I don't know how my parents finally got me to unlock my legs, but I am now living in Arizona so I must have relaxed enough to bend my knees and open the door on that little outhouse on that crisp fall evening in 1937.

ODE TO THE OUTBACK

By Gail Larson Toerpe

When I was little I used to sit
On a hardwood plank with a hole in it.

Planks that were split from a giant oak
Made a lusty wood that a guy could soak.

Only eight foot high and four foot wide
Our *convenience* shanty was just outside.

Come springtime mud or winter sleet
We done our duty in our shack retreat.

Under midnight black or skies of blue
Friends, foes 'n family skipped to the loo.

A moon-like slit and a distant smell
Recycle time to the farm in the dell.

Farewell to days in the privy line
When I took my seat where the sun don't shine.

FAR CRY

By Maggie Windsor

When World War II was over and the servicemen came home, there was a critical shortage of housing in most cities in the country. For a while, my husband and I lived with relatives in a three-bedroom house in St. Louis County, Missouri, but crowded conditions soon took their toll.

We had looked all over the city for a place to live, but there was nothing. Finally, we found a one-car garage that had been partitioned to make two rooms, a bedroom and a kitchen. There was a cookstove and a cold water spigot. Outside, there was an outhouse. That was all.

By the time we moved there were three of us, including our beautiful daughter, Cathi, weighing seven pounds, eight ounces with blond curly hair and the bluest eyes you've ever seen. There was just enough room in the bedroom for her crib, so we took the place.

We gathered a few pieces of furniture and fit them into the rooms – a bed and dresser in the bedroom and a kitchen table and chairs in the other. For bathing on Saturday nights, a tin tub had to suffice. The concrete floor was bitterly cold in December and waves of frigid air radiated upward and engulfed us.

The outhouse was clean, but my husband wanted to make it luxurious. He strung electric wires to connect an overhead light and added a small space heater to ensure our comfort. The *piece de resistance* was a lovely polished toilet seat, stained a rich walnut. That and a new magazine rack completed the work of art.

Out in front, there was a picket fence with a gate that opened onto our sidewalk, where we hung a sign saying, *Far Cry*. The neighbors stopped to ask what it meant. All we could say was that it was a *Far Cry* from what we were used to.

For a month, we stayed there, until Cathi got pneumonia. The place was too cold for her. Then we were offered an apartment at Jefferson Barracks in the housing area. The old buildings had been converted into eight apartment units, and we were fortunate to obtain one. The place was new and clean and warm, and we couldn't have been happier, especially with the indoor bathroom. To have a nice apartment and not have to worry about Cathi was all we could ask for, and we stayed eight years.

Did I mention the sign, *Far Cry,* and what became of it? We brought it with us and hung it on the railing of our little porch.

ONE FINGER OR TWO?

By Winifred Spring

Growing up in the country in the early part of this century, as I did, outhouses were just a fact of life. There was a whole culture and etiquette connected with outhouse use that city people today might find odd but that country people of my generation recognize instantly, even though most of us have lived with indoor plumbing for years.

Outhouses became a big part of my life in 1924, when I was eight years old. My family was living in Two Rivers, Wisconsin, a town on Lake Michigan about 80 miles north of Milwaukee. In that year my father decided to give up his job as a mail carrier (in his Model T Ford) and move us to a parcel of land on the outskirts of town so he could farm. In those days carrying mail was not a steady job because you had to bid on the contract to do it, so I suppose that he thought farming would be more secure.

My father built a two-room house, a barn and an outhouse about 20 feet from the house on that property. Meanwhile my mother, four brothers and sisters and I were packing up our belongings in town.

Father kept the outhouse simple, as most country people did in those days, by digging a hole and placing the little building with a seat inside directly over the top. As the years went by, he kept saying, "This year I'll build a house with plumbing," but other things kept him busy, like building a bigger barn and tending the crops. It was a dairy and truck farm, and we grew cash crops like carrots and beets for a local canning company as well as raspberries, strawberries and flowers to sell in town.

My mother was quite unhappy that my father's chores kept him from tending to the outhouse. Eventually it got pretty smelly. My mother, who had been dismayed by his decision to move to the country, was disgusted by this but couldn't see any way out but to make a new one herself. Because I was one of the older children, I helped her. She and I panted and grunted as we dug a hole about five feet deep. We then tipped the outhouse onto a wheelbarrow, rolled it over to the new site and tipped it on top of the hole.

Using the outhouse was most comfortable in the spring or fall. In the winter you never wanted to sit down on the cold seat, and going out there at night was so cold and scary – we kids avoided it. In the summer the outhouse was surrounded by flies and was, of course, stinky. We tried to kill the smell by putting ashes and hydrated lime down the hole, but sometimes even that wasn't enough. Our kittens kept their distance but not frogs and other little animals, who would sometimes jump out at us when we opened the door to the outhouse.

The type of toilet paper varied. We kids counted ourselves lucky when there were newspapers, which were relatively soft. Our least favorite was the stiff, scratchy Sears catalog. Our family made lots of jokes about who had used what kind of toilet paper, as well as speculating about whether someone would be inside when a strong wind blew the outhouse over, which did happen from time to time.

Some families got very *upscale* with their outhouse doors and windows, decorating them with fancy cutouts or covering the inside walls and doors with wallpaper. This seemed silly to me. As far as I was concerned, these embellishments couldn't cover up the basic fact that this was an outhouse. One outhouse did impress me, though. We had relatives who lived in Mishicot, which is about ten miles north of Two Rivers, Wisconsin. They were wealthy farmers who could not only afford a three-holer but actually built a boardwalk leading to the outhouse. They also installed small steps at the entrance to make it easier for little kids to climb up. I remember feeling very special as I walked back and forth along that boardwalk.

Our country school also had an outhouse. It was a one-room school with one teacher and about 20 students, spread over eight grade levels.   The outhouse was solidly constructed, had a two-sided windbreak set at a right angle to the door to shield it, and it was kept rather nicely. Because the district could not afford a janitor, the school board members took turns cleaning the outhouse twice a year. We students were in charge of sweeping out the wood-fired heater and firing it up. As I recall, the teacher brought the toilet paper.

There were all sorts of jokes and threats about the boys peeking through the knotholes when a girl was inside, and vice versa, but when we played games like *Keep Away,* we all steered clear of the outhouse. We also joked about the system the teacher invented for student *comfort* requests. For example, if you wanted a drink of water, you would signal by holding up one finger. Two fingers meant that you needed to use the outhouse. Looking back, as a former schoolteacher and principal myself, I am surprised that this entire matter was handled as naturally and delicately as it was in that school.

Outside of class, of course, we kids would tease each other by holding up fingers and wagging them in each other's faces.   In later years, this signaling system would occasionally cause giggles when some adult in a town meeting would unintentionally – in the midst of making an important point – hold up one or two fingers.

Finally, around 1935, my parents' farm was prospering enough that we could afford to install a septic system to accommodate indoor plumbing. Like most farm families, we kept the outhouse for the hired hands, but I'm pleased to say that from then on, I enjoyed the luxury of indoor plumbing with hardly a backward glance.

THE THRONE, THE BEAR AND THE BBG

By Doris Ann Hayes

"Think the bear took the TP?" Debbie voiced what we had all been wondering.

We didn't have it. The only creature on the island big enough to walk away with our toilet paper was a good-sized, pesky black bear.

"Why would he?" Sandy asked. "It's not something to eat."

I had a flashback to an old camp skit about missing the *important papers*. At this minute there were not any more important to us. It was our last roll and we still had several days worth of travel. We had no choice but to search for it.

There were eight of us on a two-week, all-female canoe trip in the Boundary Waters Canoe Area straddling the Canada-Minnesota border. The lone male was an ugly little dog named Popcorn, our protector.

Long hours of paddling, changing camp daily, cooking all meals over a fire and enduring the elements had set us up to look for rest and comfort. We were about halfway through the trip and making good progress.

Deciding that a day of layover was in order, we found a pleasant island with all of the amenities: a great campsite, beach and a throne in the woods. This was a sign of civilization drifting closer. Named more for how it made us feel than appearances, the throne was in a clearing about an eighth of a mile from the campsite. The clearing was high and had a view that would be the envy of any waterfront estate. The throne itself was built of rough wood on top of a ten-inch platform above ground level. It had a huge lid that covered the entire top of the box.

It was a real open-air outhouse. The builders felt that walls and roof were superfluous for campers in the wild. Who was there to see you sitting on the throne, anyway?

Once you got past the feeling of being really conspicuous, it was a wonderfully freeing experience to feel the breeze and watch canoeists paddling by on their way to the next portage. There was a secret pleasure in seeing and listening without being seen, and at the same time, taking care of business.

Since no one else inhabited the island, we left our toilet paper conveniently on the lid for each of us to find in turn. We were saved from carrying the TP around and it was safely ensconced in a plastic bag to ensure its dryness.

It's amazing how quickly we nested. We relaxed around the campfire that night and after taking care to hang up the food and put out the fire, we went to bed with the complacent attitude of one who does not have to go anywhere in the morning. We eight women slept the well-deserved, sound sleep of those who had earned it.

At first light, we awoke to the shouts of our guide threatening a black bear, insulting him and his relations so loudly that he quickly retreated to the bush.

We were uneasy and insisted on going in twos to the throne, made a lot of noise to be sure he was gone and went industriously about the job of making breakfast.

Afterward, the warm sun and full tummies had us returning to complacency as quickly as a boomerang returns to an expert. The sun burned off the early mist and our residual fears. We slipped right back into vacation mode.

"Guess who's coming to breakfast?" someone shouted at the bear's reappearance.

Everything erupted at once in that speedy, chaotic fashion that the movie director in our brain slows to a slow-motion, freeze-frame study.

Pots and pans were grabbed and banged. Voices rang out all around. Popcorn, the dog, made a good football substitute as the guide caught him on his way to attack the bear and tossed him to me in one smooth motion. Though he was only six inches high, he considered our protection his job. Barking orders the guide hollered, "In the tent! Get him in the tent." So in the tent we sat and prayed. Once more the bear left, with reluctance.

The fact the our bruin neighbor had the nerve to demand breakfast in broad daylight with eight people present and resisted leaving even in the face of loud confusion eliminated any doubt or indecision. We knew we had to leave and *now*. He would be back.

Immediately, without discussion, we broke camp. Quickly, as if of one mind, we repacked, loaded canoes, checked for litter and made one last trip to the throne. Our aim was to retrieve the *important papers,* our toilet paper.

It was gone. We did not know if the bear took the toilet paper but the vision of using leaves for days sent us in circles searching. Finally, we discovered it about 200 feet down a path, discarded under some thick bushes.

Twenty minutes later we gathered in our canoes. We drifted about a hundred yards offshore, able to talk peacefully for the first time that morning and examine the toilet paper.

It was still in plastic, no worse for wear, except for teeth marks, deep puncture wounds and missing hunks all over it. The TP hadn't just been picked up and carried—it had been chewed! The sweet smell had attracted the bear; the taste did not. He had chewed it and spit it out.

Gales of laughter rocked the canoes and drifted over the calm waters. It was fate. TP lost its name. From that day to this, none of us can visit an outhouse or look at a roll of tissue without thinking of BBG or Bear Bubble Gum.

MOONING OF THE OUTHOUSE

By Gail Larson Toerpe

I must admit that I never actually saw a crescent moon carved into an outhouse door in nearly twenty years of camping. Nor did I ever see one in the Wisconsin farm country of my aunt and uncle many years ago. We might deduce, therefore, that the crescent image isn't really as old as we originally thought in spite of the fact that most people accept the *mooning* as a given.

The concept of the outhouse moon was possibly created and perpetuated by generations of cartoonists. The most prominent example I can think of is Al Capp, who drew "Li'l Abner."

There *is* a reference to the odd door carvings in a book called, "The Little Red Schoolhouse: A Sketchbook of Early American Education," by Eric Sloane. Regarding 18th-and 19th-century schoolhouses he writes:

"The woodshed was often a lean-to attached to the schoolhouse, but the most accepted arrangement was to place it between the schoolhouse and the privy, with a fence separating the boys' entrance from the girls'. The ancient designation of privy doors was to saw into them a sun (for boys' toilet) and a moon (for girls' toilet)."

Mr. Sloane included a sketch of both versions, with the now-familiar quarter-moon assigned to females and the sun earmarked for males...a rather neat way, I think, to divvy the privy sheds, considering the fact that the moon is said to represent the feminine power of the "Mother Goddess, Queen of Heaven," while the sun has been seen as masculine. Many people were illiterate in the years before indoor plumbing, so some kind of visual representation of mens' room and ladies' room was necessary. The reason for carving rather than painting the signs is simple; They're meant to vent.

129

COME ON, 'NAKES

By Frank E. Konieska

Aunt Martha was a control freak. Even at the ripe old age of four, I knew this fact above all else. My four older sisters considered me spoiled; my younger one was only one year old, so she didn't count. My mother was busy with the baby, so taking care of me fell to my older sisters and Aunt Martha.

Living on a farm in the big woods of northern Wisconsin, we had the privilege of growing up reading the Sears catalog in the semidarkness of the family two-holer. When you have the two-hole deluxe model, you can use one hole, and watch down the other hole for porcupines and other wildlife who come to investigate the pungent and overpowering odors that emanate from under the outhouse.

One day while I was perusing the meaning of life and keeping a watchful eye out for an overfriendly porcupine that had been seen in the area, I saw movement in the vast underground cavern that a little four year old could fall into with very little effort if he did not hang on to both sides of the bench seat. Leaning as far over to my right as I could, I waited. What was it? Should I finish up now, or be brave and wait it out? Holding my breath, I spied movement again. It was a big garter snake, probably a poisonous, deadly one. These are rare but not unheard of.

A flash of inspiration and the beginning of an idea started growing in my mind. As with any idea a four year old gets, it soon became the most important thing in the world. The world being in balance, I had found the yin for Aunt Martha's yang. Snakes were the only thing I knew she was afraid of.

If I could put her and some snakes together in the confined space of the outhouse, I might be able to teach her to fear me. Everyone else had to do what she said, but it would be different with me.

First, to plant the seeds. Running up to the house, I told everyone who was willing to listen about the big snake I had seen under the outhouse. I guess I had to tell everybody about it a few times before they would believe me. I don't remember how many days everyone avoided the place as much as possible, or went in twos for protection, but finally Aunt Martha was on her way down the path to her eventual fate of being terrorized and possibily bitten by snakes.

Lurking in the dark places, behind and between the trees along the path, I followed her as she slowly searched the path—both sides, ahead and, once in a while, the trees above—for possible reptiles. Showing an amazing amount of control, she calmly walked down the garden path. When she reached the end and slowly opened the outhouse door, I could see her trying to make up her mind whether it was safe to go in or if it was better to just forget the whole thing.

Seems she decided that leaving the door open would be the safest thing. I gave her enough time to get inside, settle down and get comfortable. Sneaking up on the side so she couldn't see me, I reached around and slowly pushed the door closed. Reaching up, I turned the latch closed and leaned against the door. Taking a deep breath, I started hollering and calling for the snakes. "Here 'nakes,…here nakes,…here nakes. I've got her. Come get her. Here 'nakes. Here nakes."

With what sounded like the snorting and the stamping of a bull, Aunt Martha hit the floor. A second later she was trying to shoulder the door open. I don't know how a small boy and that flimsy door latch could hold her in, but the more she shouted and banged on the door, the more afraid I was to let go and the more I hollered for the snakes. She had that outhouse rocking so bad I thought it was going to fall over on me.

In her panic, she was probably running into the walls, but after a couple of minutes, I knew the snakes either

131

weren't coming or wouldn't get there in time to keep me from being killed if she made it through the door. It was time for plan B.

Taking another deep breath, I pushed away from the door and ran up the path and out into the cornfield. I was short enough that I could run between the rows without showing any movement on the surface. Once into the woods on the other side, I determined to spend the rest of my life hiding under the fern forest. This was my favorite private refuge and no one ever found me there. I could lay there and listen to the world go on around me.

So started a lifetime of running away from Aunt Martha, for one reason or another. She didn't kill me over the 'nake incident, and even found it cute to tell the story in later years. I've never forgiven the stupid snakes for not showing up when I needed them, and I guess it's only fair that I have nightmares and a mortal fears of snakes to this day.

THE SMOKING PARLOR

By Jerry Goudy

As an eleven year old in Nebraska in the early 1940's my friends and I were a pretty sophisticated lot. We were farm boys who were plenty smart around farm machinery, horses and cattle. There wasn't anything we couldn't do. Why, we even smoked. The brands of choice were confined to what was available - corn silk or coffee grounds or milk weed silks all wrapped in toilet paper or tissue.

We also knew where to smoke without getting caught and never smoked behind the barn. We were sure our parents never knew. We were just too clever.

One day I was visiting my friend Ardith. The late summer sun was hot and we were tired of playing.

"I have a match and some corn silk in my pocket," I said. "Should we roll a couple?"

"Sure," Ardith replied. "Dad's in the field and Mom's busy canning. The rest of the family is visiting friends or in the field helping Dad. We can smoke in the outhouse. No one will ever know."

It was a great idea. The outhouse was a two-holer, so it would not be crowded with both of us in it. Also, there was a slight breeze and the smoke smell would dissipate quickly.

The coast was clear as we slipped in the door and blocked it shut. The half moon on the door and the space between the wall and the roof afforded enough light to roll our cigarettes. I hung mine on my lip and lit Ardith's. After I lit my own, I casually tossed the match down the hole.

Whooooosh!

The next thing we knew we heard the roar of fire as flames shot half a foot out of one of the holes. Not being well versed on the presence of hydrogen and hydrogen sulfide, we thought we'd set the outhouse on fire. We dropped our cigarettes and raced to the horse tank. It was about a half a block from the outhouse, but at the time it seemed like miles. Somewhere along the way we grabbed a five-gallon bucket and flung it into the tank as soon as we got close enough. Before it had a chance to fill, we yanked it out and ran. It was too heavy for one of us to carry even partially full. As we ran with the bucket between us, we about yanked each other's arms off besides drenching each other. Fortunately, there was enough water left to pour on the fire, which had subsided on its own. The smell was awful as we emptied the bucket down the hole.

Our return trip was less frantic. When we were sure the fire was out, we tried to destroy any evidence of our little escapade.

We never heard a word about it, but I'm sure Ardith's parents told mine and they must have had a good laugh over the antics of their young sons. The experience certainly dampened our enthusiasm for smoking.

MY FIRST TIME

By Tricia Sanders

I can remember the morning my mom asked if I wanted to spend the weekend at my aunt's farm. The memory lingers like it was yesterday. I was ecstatic. It was only Tuesday, but I started packing and was finished before I went to bed that evening. The rest of the week dragged on. I was going to the farm.

I envisioned horses, cows, chickens, barns, tractors and almost every other image a farm conjures up. I could see myself getting up each morning before dawn and going to milk the cows with my uncle or gathering eggs from the chicken house with my aunt. My imagination also had me riding a tall black stallion with my hair billowing in the breeze.

On Saturday, the long ride was not merely an inconvenience but a painful waste of time. It took an hour and a half to get to the farm. I had never been before. My aunt and uncle had moved to the farm just a few short months before, leaving behind their city house that was much like mine – nothing extraordinary, just a three- bedroom house on a street in a neighborhood – no comparison to a farm.

In addition to my aunt and uncle, my three girl cousins lived on the farm. The oldest was five years older than me; the middle one was my age, eight; and the youngest was only two. How lucky they were. I imagined all the times when they could take baby animals to school for show-and-tell or ride ponies instead of bikes.

When we arrived at the farm, my aunt had dinner waiting. In the middle of the table was a platter of fried chicken like none I had ever seen. It was overflowing with chicken. The mashed potatoes, gravy and homemade biscuits made me wish I lived on a farm. After dinner, Mom and Dad made the trek back to the city while I helped the cousins wash dishes. They had to pump a big handle to get water to come in the sink. It looked really hard. Finally the water came in spurts, but not into the sink. They had a big pan waiting to catch the water. After it was full, they put it on the stove to heat it up. I remember thinking it was really strange that they didn't have hot water coming out of the pump.

While my cousins were waiting for the water to heat up, I went looking for the bathroom. On the first floor there was a kitchen; a living room with a big round, black stove; and a bedroom. Near the staircase was a door I assumed would be the bathroom. It wasn't. It was a closet. I decided the bathroom must be upstairs, so I climbed up with a little urgency, because by this time I had to go. At the top of the stairs were two more bedrooms, but no bathroom.

I figured I'd overlooked it and went back downstairs. As I was going down my aunt was coming up.

"I need to go to the bathroom, but I can't find it." I said.

She got a really funny look on her face and started laughing.

"We don't have a bathroom in the house. Go downstairs and tell one of the girls to take you out back to the outhouse."

"Outhouse, what's that?" I asked.

"It's our bathroom, but it is not in the house."

I continued downstairs thinking they must really be fancy to have a whole separate house for their bathroom.

When I told my cousins I had to go to the bathroom, the two older ones wrinkled their noses. The oldest one, Sissy, pointed to Linda, the middle one, and said, "You take her. I'm not going out there."

"I ain't takin' her. You take her."

By this time, I was not in the mood to hear any more arguing. I had to go to the bathroom, and I was fairly certain I could do it by myself.

"Just show me where it is. I have to go," I pleaded.

Sissy pointed out the back door to the little wooden building next to the shed. It sure looked awfully little for a bathroom, but I had to go, so off I went. The closer I came to the little building the more aware I was of the pungent odor. I remember thinking it must be awfully close to the pigpen.

The building was made of old, weathered wood and it leaned a little. The door was held in place by two rusty hinges on one side and a similar-looking latch on the other. There was a little white knob that served as the door handle. I grabbed the knob and yanked the door open. The hideous smell hit me right smack in the face. It smelled like something had died. The stench was so overwhelming it was all I could do to keep from heaving.

I blinked to see into the tiny room. Sunlight was trying to get in through a side window, but it wasn't having much luck. The window was streaked and grimy with age. I peered around looking for the toilet, but all I could see was a wooden bench with a hole in the top, and on top of that hole was a toilet lid. I wasn't quite sure what I had found but I was fairly certain it was not the bathroom. On the wall next to the bench was a piece of bent wire hanging on a nail with a roll of toilet paper hanging from it. At the base of the bench was a step stool. I was in the bathroom! This was the most disgusting place I had ever been in.

I moved closer to the bench/toilet just as the door squeaked closed behind me. Suddenly the room was plunged into darkness, except for the few rays of light filtering in the dirty, cobweb-infested window. I started out the door and saw my cousins standing on the back porch, laughing. They would just love it if their citified cousin was a big pansy. Instead I turned around and let the door close behind me. It took a few minutes for my eyes to adjust to the darkness, but when they did, I climbed up the stool and raised the lid. The smell was unbearable. I wasn't quite sure what was down there, and I sure wasn't going to look. I did my business as best I could without touching anything.

At the house, I walked past my cousins feeling rather smug. I wasn't quite sure how I would endure the rest of the weekend, not convinced riding horses and milking cows would make up for the lack of bathroom facilities.

The next morning I woke up long before daylight. My cousins were still both sound asleep. Surely one of them would wake up soon. My bladder was about to burst, but I was not about to go outside by myself. I could see out the window and it was pitch black, no streetlights like at home. One hour dragged into the next and still no one budged. The light was just barely creeping over the windowsill, when I heard someone padding down the hall.

I prayed it would be my aunt. She peeked in the door, and I made my break.

"I have to go to the bathroom really bad," I whispered. She led me down to her bedroom and slid a little ceramic jar out from under the bed.

"Here, this is a chamber pot. We use this at night, so we don't have to go outside," she said.

Before the weekend was over, I had decided the farm was pretty neat. I learned to ride a horse, milk a cow, and the most important thing – make sure I used the bathroom every time we went to town!

THE PRESIDENT'S PROPRIETY

By Vernette F. Fulop

As we sped along Interstate 75 returning home from a conference in Atlanta, we saw on the map that we were near the road leading to Plains, Georgia, President Jimmy Carter's hometown. We knew it was a small town from what we'd heard and read, but not this small. Main Street stores filled one block - on one side of the street.

After checking out the museum in the old high school and several other buildings like Jimmy Carter's brother's gas station and the two churches, and finding a delicious lunch in the tiny old bank building, we wanted to see the president's old homestead farm. A couple miles out of town we found it and it was like farms I was used to visiting as a child: a windmill, white frame farmhouse, not too big and not too small. The rooms were not spacious but comfortable for an average American family. The barns had been restored and the pecan groves he and his father tended were still there.

One small building on the side of the house was a food supply shop for the neighbors and former sharecroppers. In between was an unusual setup of a tennis court, with raked smooth brown soil 'and painted lines with the usual net. The park ranger said that was quite unusual for a farm, and said Jimmy's father insisted the children learn to play tennis.

Just as we were about to leave, we passed a small brown building at the back of the house. I looked at it as we went by and the ranger said, "Yup, that's the outhouse. And you see the door faces away from the house. When it was restored, Jimmy came checking one day as he often did and said that it wasn't right. The outhouse door faced the house and that was improper." So the workmen had to dig up the cement base and turn it around. The old restored outhouse of the Carter family farm had to be properly placed with the door facing *away* from the house.

THE GAUNTLET

By Mario Del Rosso

When I first met my wife, she lived on an old farmstead outside Sussex, Wisconsin. Though the family didn't farm, it had all the requisite parts left from the old days – small barn, apple orchard, small farm animals and the outhouse, complete with crescent moon carved in the door. No matter that there was no central heating or that the water source was a well in the yard, it was a cozy, love-filled home for the family. The main drawback came when *nature* called.

It was bad enough to endure a visit to the outhouse in winter. All processes were speeded up so as little time as absolutely necessary was wasted in our haste to get back to the warmth of the potbellied stove in the parlor. The footprint trail in the snow got pretty well packed down and overshoes were needed only when a new snowfall filled the trail. The worst drawback came when the geese were in the yard.

Usually, the flock stayed close to the barn, but occasionally they wandered into the yard by the outhouse. This caused no trouble as long as that facility was not in use. The geese, after all, made great watchdogs. No one could approach the house without them raising an unholy racket with their quacking and honking. This was fine until you had to make use of the outhouse. Then you had to *run the gauntlet.*

The hens were trouble enough, rushing you with wings outstretched trying to beat you and with beaks at the ready to nip you while they hissed loudly at your intrusion into their space. But the gander was even worse. Bigger and fearless, he would rush you directly. The only way to avoid him was to take a broom along to fend him off while you made a beeline to the john. On the way out, when your outhouse business was complete, the process had to be repeated until you were safe back in the house.

Most of the family was used to this charade, but my wife was not. The gander seemed to sense her fear and was even more belligerent to her than to the rest of us. He had her so afraid of him that only on the severest call of nature would she dare venture out the back door into his domain alone. So it fell to me to be Lancelot and escort my Guinevere past the gander-dragon on her mission. Armed with my broom-lance, I went forth to do battle with the monster to clear the way.

Honking and hissing, he rushed me head-on. I deftly jabbed him with one motion while stepping aside. By the time he turned I was close enough to actually push him backward, affording the opening Jean was looking for. She raced toward the safety of the crescent-carved door while I stood guard lest the beast attack again. The process was repeated on the way back to the house.

Many years have passed since we last used that old backyard facility. More modern plumbing has alleviated the need for fighting your way to a toilet where you froze your bottom in winter and sweltered in summer. The size of the seats is now standardized and the Sears catalog is out of vogue. And yet, the memory of the old days in the outhouse lingers --- like a scent does in the still August air--- distinctive and not entirely unpleasant.

THE HOSTAGE

By Nancy Burns
As told to: Joy Ross

Tommy's mother died when he was two weeks old. He had two older brothers and a sister. Tommy's father felt he could manage the three older children, but he knew nothing about caring for an infant. So Tommy's maternal grandmother and his mother's three young unmarried sisters offered to take Tommy and raise him. His father really didn't have a choice, plus he felt it would be the best for Tommy, so he agreed.

From the moment Tommy came to live with the four women in Mill Creek, West Virginia, his every whim was catered to. Whatever Tommy wanted, Tommy got.

Helen, the youngest of his three aunts, got her certificate to teach school when Tommy, a big redheaded boy, was eight years old. The family celebrated with a party for Helen. Tommy also got a present—a new BB gun. He'd already worn out the one he had and was known throughout the community as a good shot. Tommy was thrilled to get the new gun because his goal was to be the best marksman in West Virginia.

When Helen received her first paycheck, she gave Tommy a generous portion of it because he wanted a new bicycle. However, the money she gave him wasn't quite enough for the new bike. He asked for more, but she refused, whereupon Tommy pitched a cat fit. Helen was unmoved by his theatrics, so Tommy stormed out of the house yelling, "I'll get you for this!"

On the next Saturday afternoon, Tommy's grandmother and two older aunts went to town. Tommy was still sulking and wouldn't go, and Helen wanted to work on a dress she was making.

About thirty minutes after the others left for town, Helen felt the call of nature and went to the outhouse out behind the house. As she opened the door when she was finished with her business and tried to come out, she heard a sharp "Ping!" Something hit the outside handle. Startled, Helen jumped back. *Must have been one of the hickory nuts falling from the tree*, she thought.

Again she pushed on the door to open it. Once again, "Ping!" The same thing happened. Helen got concerned. "Who's there?" she called.

"I told you I'd get you," Tommy yelled at her. "I've got you trapped and I'm not going to let you out."

"Stop that this minute, Tommy!" Helen yelled at her young nephew.

"No!"

"Please, Tommy, it's hot in here, and it smells bad."

Helen tried to open the door and another BB hit the handle. She begged and pleaded, cried and cajoled, all to no avail. Helen was trapped and she knew it. She screamed until she was hoarse.

The standoff lasted three hours and didn't end until the others returned from town and heard Helen's weak cries and rescued her.

Tommy was scolded as Helen retreated to her room, sick from the noxious outhouse fumes.

When Tommy grew up and became the head of the highway patrol, he was often asked, "What's the worst thing you've ever done in your life?" He always replied, "Oh, that would have to be the time I held my poor Aunt Helen hostage for three hours in the outdoor privy."

LESSONS FROM THE FARMYARD

By Darlene Hoggard Davis

"How do you stay so skinny?"
The new son-in-law wanted to know.
Maw sweetly smiled and said, "Just turkey."
The son-in-law mumbled, "Oh."

"Where is your bathroom?
He asked her folks and grinned.
"Out in the farmyard," the family said.
He looked a little chagrined.

He opened the gate and walked to the shed,
Stepped up to the seat and sat down.
The whole family came out to watch the show;
It was better than going to town.

He sang out a song about Barnacle Bill
And another about his sweet mom.
When he opened the door, he was knocked down
By a 40-pound turkey named Tom.

Instantly, he knew, why his wife was so thin
And her family laughed with such glee.
No time to think now-he had to get up.
He had to outrun the devil and flee.

Tom Turkey didn't like strangers in his yard.
Ruffled his feathers, you might say.
As he tenderized the fellow, flogging calves and butt,
You could hear the son-in-law loudly pray.

"Lord, you know I couldn't 'go' when I got here today;
All I could do was pee.
Get me back to the privy now, Lord. And thank You-
This turkey's scared the crap out of me!"

My dad learned lessons that day on Grandpaw's farm,
Lessons he never forgot:
The Lord surely works in mysterious ways
And He can even teach the lame to Turkey Trot.

THE DAY THEY MOVED THE JOHN INDOORS

By John McCollister

Progress? You be the judge. It all began one frosty morning with the temperature cloistered below the zero mark for the umpteenth consecutive day. The flannel-draped body of a determined woodsman followed a well-trodden path from the secure warmth of his fishing cabin in the woods to the not-so-inviting depository known in the vernacular as the *outdoor john.*

Only minutes before, while lying under the protection of his feathered quilt, he'd had a personal debate as to whether or not he should brave the jaunt of 25 yards. Secretly, he hoped the urge would vanish -- at least until it warmed-up five degrees or so. Ah, but such was not the case. The consequences of a bologna sandwich, three dill pickles, a giant scoop of ice cream and four bottles of beer consumed within a three-hour period the night before were taking revenge. He decided to complete the drastic ordeal as quickly as possible.

Urged on by the penetrating chill that awoke every nerve ending, he hurried toward the half-mooned door, only to discover the ice that had formed across the base held the wood secure. One desperate yank (with expletive deleted) did the trick.

There, in the early morning light, were the proverbial two seats -- the bedrock of America. This was where a part-time custodian of a ghetto school could sit beside a successful New York CEO and be equal.

This was where those who graced these seats engaged in sophisticated dialogue covering a multitude of subjects ranging from situational ethics to the increasing price of a hot dog at a baseball game. But now was not the time to meditate on tradition.

Our friend completed his predawn task and hastened back to his cabin without bothering to button completely the back flap, now stiff from the frozen froth which two months ago had been air.

Cursing a minced oath, he slid back into the cocoon of his downy mattress. "Tomorrow," he swore, "I'm gonna move that !?!&#! bathroom indoors."

Later that morning, he weaved his way through the peaceful forest to the nearest town to make the necessary arrangements.

A contractor was called. He in turn notified a team of plumbers, a carpenter and a tax assessor.

The contractor was able to drive the country road to the entrance of the hunting paradise and follow the two-mile path to the cabin. However, this was impossible for the carpenter who had to have a roadway wide enough for his truck and assorted tools.

Consequently, bulldozers were rented in order to begin the task of felling oaks, pines and elms that had adorned the countryside for centuries.

Two weeks were spent clearing the way. The carpenter, oblivious to the smothering of nature's greenery, spent an entire 30 minutes measuring the spot for the proposed john transplant. The estimated cost of his labor and materials was astronomical. "It's hard to get wood these days," he uttered.

The caravan of plumbers was summoned. More problems. Although the new road was wide enough, the heavy trucks could not be driven on dirt paths. After all, it might rain, and the equipment would be mired in this forsaken retreat.

There was only one answer: The road had to be asphalted. Several weeks and more bulldozers later, a slick, two-lane road parted the remaining trees to transport the plumbers with enough gadgets to erect suitable facilities for an overflow crowd at Shea Stadium.

Nails were driven, pipes compressed, bowls fitted and water primed.

The carpenter finished the inside paneling, while the contractor totaled the bill. (The tax assessor had camped in the third bunk from the door five hours after the first call.)

Proud of his new convenience, our brave woodsman invited the townspeople for a grand opening. Mayor Fitzsimmons presided over the ribbon-cutting. The local rag sent its ace reporter and camera to cover the event. It was Christmas, Thanksgiving, Fourth of July and a bar mitzvah all rolled into one.

News of this project reached the sister of the mayor, a second cousin to the brother-in-law of the state's lieutenant governor. She passed the word to the chambers of the state capitol where, in the midst of a Senate debate on legalized abortion, the lieutenant governor heard of his distant relative's husband's ribbon-cutting ceremony for the highway to the john now moved indoors.

The heated debate had the lieutenant governor worried. The fact the governor was Roman Catholic didn't help matters. Everyone needed a break.

The Lieutenant Governor strongly suggested that he and few of his colleagues travel north (at taxpayers' expense) to see this eighth wonder of the world located in their own backyard.

That Saturday afternoon, as the leaves were beginning to display their spring coats, an assembled party of 59 senatorial souls journeyed to the secluded woods via the newly paved road to the mecca in the wilderness.

"A superb sight," growled Senator Quigly.

"Indeed it is," answered the burly lieutenant governor.

"But, isn't it a pity that the trees had to be removed?" offered a junior senator.

The lieutenant governor frowned noticeably. "Do you want to stop progress, boy?"

"Uh…no sir.

"Harrumph...It's too bad all our fair citizens cannot partake of this offering of nature."

"Precisely what I was thinking," said the junior senator.

"Harrumph," said the lieutenant governor. "Take a note. Suggest that we place this property under eminent domain. Our people must have the chance to see what we are seeing. Above all, it must be first-class work."

"First-class work!" said the senator.

"First-class work!" cried the assembled body in unison.

And first-class work it was.

Gone was the asphalt two-mile driveway. In its stead sprawled a four-lane freeway with a central median. Along both sides of the road were gigantic signs that read: "DON'T LITTER. SAVE OUR COUNTRYSIDE."

Gone, too, were the fish and deer, birds and flowers, clean air and silent retreat where the sound of a rippling brook was penetrated only by the splash of a nearby trout.

In short, gone was the chance for secluded relaxation which our friend and his companions shared for decades.

Yet the desire lingered. Nothing would stop him from realizing his dream. So, with the money he received from the state, he purchased a homestead 75 miles farther north, consisting of one cabin with three bedrooms plus (you guessed it) one outdoor john.

Now, that's progress.

THREE LITTLE OUTHOUSE STORIES

By Nila Ridings

GIRL SCOUT CAMP CRISIS

I loved going to Girl Scout camp in the summer. I met new friends, learned new skills and enjoyed the total outdoor experience. Each day we were assigned duties to keep the camp tidy and organized. My latrine duty turned into a major disaster. We used diluted bleach and a toilet brush to scrub each facility.   Suddenly, the brush jerked and it was gone...gone to the bottom of the outhouse hole. My heart pounded. How would I explain I dropped the brush and, worse yet, how was I going to get it out? I debated one idea after another and finally decided I had no other choice. I was going to have to tell the scout leader. She assured me it was nothing to be upset over and all was fine. To this day, 40 years later, every time I smell bleach or see a toilet brush, I have flashbacks of the day the toilet brush fell into the outhouse hole, never to be seen again.

BATHROOM NEED ARISES ENROUTE TO GRANDMA'S

I was about ten years old when we were driving from Kansas City to Grandma's house in Girard, Kansas. The two-lane highway was a winding curvy thing and suddenly Mother Nature made a call. This was before the days of fast-food restaurants and convenience stores every few miles down the road. I couldn't wait much longer when suddenly my dad spotted an outhouse next to the highway. It wasn't what I had in mind, but I was at the countdown stage and jumped out of the car.

Suddenly, another more serious dilemma presented itself. No toilet paper! I looked side to side, up and down, all around, not one square to be found. What I saw was a big Sears, Roebuck catalog. I'm saying to myself, *who has time to come out here and shop the catalog but forgets to put toilet paper in this thing?*

Finally, I gave up hope and got back in the car. My parents detected my disgust and asked what was wrong. After my explanation they both burst into laughter. Of course, I found absolutely nothing funny about any of it until they told me the catalog was what they used before toilet paper was invented. *Oh great*, I thought, *my situation could have been compounded by me arriving at Grandma's with an ad for a washing machine on my butt!*

Ever since then, toilet paper is one of my favorite modern-day conveniences.

STORY FROM MY DAD

In his small Kansas town in the 1930s, my dad and his buddies decided to surprise the town folk on Halloween. They were pushing over outhouses for fun. I suppose all was going well until they pushed one over with the farmer still inside. He came out with a rifle and shot them in their backsides with buckshot. My dad had some explaining to do when he showed up at home with buckshot in his butt. His advice to me on Halloween was: If you're going to push outhouses over, make sure the door is face down.

A Moving Experience

By Karen Stiles

When I was a child growing up in Wisconsin, we had a ritual of going camping near the Minnesota border in LaCrosse every fall. My mom was not particularly thrilled with going anywhere that did not have running water and flush toilets, but she martyred her way through the experience - that is, until we visited Wildcat Mountain Campground where we stayed for our fall adventure.

This place, as can be surmised by the name, was very hilly, rocky and full of wild animals, snakes and wild children. The name of the campground alone should have been a warning, but my mom braved this trip with eight of her ten children ranging in age from two years to about age sixteen.

Mom was a trooper about using the disgusting outhouse, the only facility at the campground; that is, until the day she used the privy with several of her hoodlum children in tow.

While Mom was in the outhouse, which was perched on unstable terrain next to a plummeting bluff, my brothers, sisters and I thought how funny it would be to help our mom with a little *movement.*

Opportunities like this didn't happen too often. You didn't dare try to pull one over on Mom too often because she had an incredible backhand that she would use on our behinds if necessary. However, with her locked behind a door and her pants around her ankles, we knew we had the thrill of a lifetime right at our fingertips. By the time she could catch us, we'd be at the top of the next hill, thanks to a pretty good running start.

We waited till we knew she was properly in place and then started rocking the outhouse back and forth, back and forth. We thought we heard a camper shout, "Hey, is that a coyote?" Actually, it was just our mom screaming.

We weren't trying to be entirely cruel; I mean, we would have caught the outhouse with mom in it before it went over the bluff. But Mom, being the sharp woman she was, couldn't be too sure.

Let's just say, Mom survived and so did we. She came out of the outhouse a little whiter than when she went in, but no Ex-Lax was needed either. She found the experience to be quite *moving.*

SYMBOLS ON THE OUTHOUSE

By Dan Poynter

The West Point Parachute Team hosted an interservice military skydiving competition at its Wallkill, New York, drop zone around 1970. Being on the board of directors for the U.S. Parachute Association, New York was in my territory. So, I attended.

That airport, otherwise unused, had little more than a runway and a gravel target. For the event, the Army hauled in large, multiholed military latrine buildings on wheels. To mark the latrine genders, they used the universal medical symbols for male and female, the circle with the arrow pointing up for males and the circle with the cross underneath for females.

One crusty old master sergeant and good friend from Fort Bragg was heard to comment: "Who put the hippie peace symbols on the outhouses?"

POTTY TRAINING OUTHOUSE STYLE

By Bill and Lois Griffith

Potty training the first child is the ultimate challenge for relatively new parents. It seemed to us that the summertime would be a good time to start. The obvious reason as far as Mom was concerned: less clothes, less hassle. Paper diapers had not yet been introduced and training pants were heavy cotton garments, unlike the wonderful ones on the market today. The sooner we were out of diapers, the sooner there would be less laundry and fewer trips up and down the basement stairs.

Summer also meant it was time to visit friends and family. It also meant irregular hours for eating and sleeping, which did nothing to help the training process, but we forged ahead.

One visit on the schedule was to our cousins in the Adirondacks who owned a rustic farm at the end of a country road. Bob and Marian had done a lot to this wonderful old home, but indoor plumbing was still on the agenda. We had coped with it so far and had explained the lovely old outhouse to our son. At two-and-a-half years old, he was more interested in looking down the hole and exclaiming at the smell than using it for its intended purpose.

After lunch, we were helping to clear the table and wash dishes when we realized our child was missing. A glance out the kitchen window gave us a clue as to where he might be.

Strung across the backyard was a pair of little sneakers, two socks, a pair of shorts, the hated training pants and a little striped shirt. As we came out the back door and around the corner, there was our child, stark naked, sitting in the outhouse with the door wide open, singing to the birds. Not wanting to alarm him and have him fall down the hole, which was quite a bit bigger than he was, we casually sauntered up to the outhouse and asked if he was finished. He looked up and said, "I go potty."

Dr. Spock would never believe this, but after that, potty training was over. The thrill of the outhouse had done the trick. If we'd known that, we would have visited the Adirondacks sooner.

The No-Walls, No-Stalls Outhouse

By Charlotte Steinzig

I've lived in the coastal mountain range in the Bay area of California since 1969. For most of those years, until 1996, we did not have an indoor bathroom in our rustic home built in the hillside of a tiny place called Canyon, California. And yet, I didn't have an outhouse either. Not really. It simply couldn't be called a "house" because there were no walls. There was a "rooflet" made of two-by-four supports holding up a roof made of plywood covered with roofing material. If it was raining, this was more than enough to keep a person dry.

Our outside toilet was located quite a few yards from the house, back up the ravine and up the steep steps cut into the rocky hillside and then a bit of a trail. The structure itself was simply a large platform, about six feet by four feet. It sat snugly on a huge hole dug by my two sons, Benjamin and Canyon, deep and wide, cut into the rock of these California hills made of shale, sandstone, clay.

This is California, the coastal range. We are not in the high Sierra Nevadas, where an outhouse is a lovely walk from the cabin across a meadow and in the winter there's so much snow that the outhouse is probably half-buried by it. I've been in a number of outhouses over the many years, up in the mountains for example. They were all the same. Dark and home to a variety of spiders, beetles and bad literature.

No, I did not have an outhouse as such. Our outdoor toilet was open, no sides, no beetles, no darkness, no bad literature, no catalogs. From the open-air seat, I could look across the ravine, watch a Steller's jay, hear an owl or listen very carefully for a deer making its way down, only to hear it stop when it realized that someone was too close, albeit someone sitting very still, on a platform, over a hole dug in the ground, set back in the trees, in dappled light.

I love my new indoor modern bathroom. I love it every day. It's very small and looks like it belongs in a motel. People who come to visit are pleased with it. I look up at the old outside toilet and recall that at some point in the 1800s, a town in Maryland passed a local ordinance banning the new contraption called a flush toilet. The town fathers spoke out against it as both foul and unsanitary. I can't say that I don't agree with them. And I know that my kids would all agree. Just think about it. A tightly sealed outhouse built within your home.

Whenever I look up toward that structure out in the woods, which is still there, I think that open-aired throne is actually nicer, smarter, cleaner, good. Then I think about my new indoor modern bathroom: convenient. What a trade-off. But there we have it.

WHAT I LEARNED
AT THE OUTHOUSE RACES

By Patricia Lorenz

My father, Ed Kobbeman, from the small town of Rock Falls in northern Illinois, whose picture is on the cover of this book, is one of the all-time-great, get-it-done, do-it-now, kind of guys. Born in 1919, he was a fighter pilot in World War II. In 1947, after the war ended, he built his own home, a three-bedroom ranch where he still lives today. That house is a veritable showplace of repair and improvement. He's often out in the barn fixing things before they break, restoring antiques, cars, farm wagons or tractors. Or he's building things from scratch or designing and creating amazing gadgets and gizmos.

It wasn't too surprising when, in 1994, Dad proudly showed me his latest creation...the outhouse he'd built from the rough wood ripped from an old wooden crate. The traditional sun and moon were cut through the front door. The sloped roof had shake shingles. Dad had fashioned a fancy seat inside, within arm's reach of course to the supply of corn cobs dangling on strings. The dual-purpose Sears, Roebuck catalog hung from a hook on one of the inside walls. There was even an American flag waving off the back end. It was, indeed, a fine outhouse.

Why a man, who built an all-electric home in the 1940s with a beautiful modern bathroom, would build an outhouse in the 1990s was something of a puzzle to me at first until Dad explained that he intended to enter his creation in the Annual Rock Falls Days Outhouse Races.

To be in this grand event, one's outhouse had to have wheels. Those he found in his neat-as-a-pin storage area outside the barn, taken off some old contraption he'd worked on years before.

The day of the race, Dad's nephews, the outhouse racing team, arrived to load up his pride and joy into their pickup truck. The four team members and one great-niece weighing in at under a hundred pounds who was chosen to ride in the seat inside, per race rules, were all wearing red look-alike, tank-style, T-shirts. They looked so spiffy they could have been vying for a medal at the outhouse event at the Summer Olympics.

The contraption arrived safely into the heart of downtown Rock Falls. In the blazing sun of that scorching June day, the five outhouse teams lined up. The four muscular nephews in charge of the Kobbeman outhouse grabbed the pole handles and rocked ole Bessy back and forth. Team unity solidified as the red-chested nephews chanted before their race with destiny, "Feel da rhythm, hear da rhyme, come on team, it's outhouse time!"

The starting shot rang out. The red-shirted Kobbeman clan, out in front by a foot, screeched around the markers 30 yards down the parking lot and turned 180 degrees to make their way back to the start/finish line.

Just then, disaster. The hard rubber on the wheels started peeling off. One at a time, hardened black tires split off the wheels as old rubber gave way to new asphalt. The nephews hung on for the last few feet, barely winning the first race by sheer strength of will and brute muscle power as they lifted that outhouse off the ground, niece and all, and drag-carried her across the finish line. But now there was no hope for the second heat.

I stood there, ready to cry. My father had put so much time and talent into making what was obviously the most superior outhouse there, and now it was all over. Without wheels an outhouse cannot run.

Out of the corner of my eye I saw Dad walking like a madman away from the race. I wondered if he was as disgusted with those old tires as I. *What a shame*, I thought, *to lose the contest because of some stupid old wheels.*

Considering the strength and enthusiasm of the red-chested manpower, it was a low blow, indeed.

Five minutes later I realized Dad hadn't come back. *Where is he?* I thought apprehensively. Thinking he'd gone off to the rest room at the corner tap, I suddenly realized that if he didn't get back soon he'd miss the rest of the races.

Minutes ticked by. By now my cousins were using the old standby, gray duct tape, to wrap the wheels in hopes that they could patch them together tight enough to at least try for the second race.

Five minutes later Dad was still nowhere to be seen. *Doggone, him*, I thought. *Where could he be? Gone off, upset at himself for using old tires on a new outhouse? How could he just leave like that? This was my Dad, for heaven's sake, the man who spent a great deal of my childhood teaching me to be a good sport, to enjoy life, but to always play the game fairly. And now, just because the wheels fell off his outhouse he's acting like a poor sport? He could have at least stuck around to see if the patched-up, wobbly tires would work in the next race.*

The announcer was on the microphone telling the participants to get their outhouses lined up. Just then Dad ran up to outhouse row, clutching four brand-new wheels. He tossed me a few tools.

"Here, hold these. Hand me those needle-nose pliers."

Within seconds the nephews and Dad had that wooden, shake-shingled wonder on its back, ripping the duct tape off with the pliers, undoing rusty nuts and bolts and attaching the brand-new wheels. It was a scene straight out of the pit at the Indy 500. Fifty seconds flat and those new wheels were in place.

The starting gun blasted through that steam heat summer day and they were off!

The Kobbeman clan won the next four races amid plenty of good-natured hooting and hollering from the folks on the sidelines. In the ceremony that followed, Dad and his nephews and great-niece were presented with an outhouse

160

trophy so spectacular that it could only be given to the finest of privy makers. That shiny, blue-and-gold, two-foot-tall trophy even had a tiny little outhouse on top with the door wide open, as if to say, "Come on in, friend!"

After the presentation, photo session and lots of backslapping and congratulatory kudos from the townspeople, including the mayor, we headed home. In the car I asked Dad, "Where'd you go when you ran off like that? And where'd you get those new wheels?"

My father, who was just two months shy of his 75th birthday, took a deep breath.

"Well," he said, starting slowly, then speeding up his words as he told the story, "I ran two-and-a-half blocks to the car. Unlocked it, drove home like a bat out of Bangkok, two miles, ran in the house, got the key to the barn, ran out there, unlocked the barn, pulled my new lawn mower out on the grass, grabbed some tools, pulled off the first two wheels, and threw 'em in the car. Then I decided I could take the other two off downtown while the boys were puttin' the first two on the outhouse. So I lifted that lawn mower into the back end of the station wagon. Then I decided that was dumb. I could take the wheels off there at home just as fast, so I lifted the lawn mower back out of the car and unbolted the second pair of wheels, threw 'em in the car, put the lawnmower back in the barn, locked the door, jumped in the car, drove back to town and just happened to find a parking place right in front of the start of the race. Must have been a guardian angel. Best luck I ever had findin' a parking place."

I couldn't believe my ears. "Dad, you did all that in the fifteen minutes you were gone, between race number one and race number two?"

"Yup."

I just shook my head.

"Why? Why did you do all that in this heat? You had a heart attack ten years ago, remember? And how did you know you wouldn't just miss all the rest of the races when you took off for home like that?"

He smiled. "Well, I just couldn't let the boys down. They worked so hard to win that first race, I just couldn't let those old rotten wheels ruin their chances for the rest of the races. Besides, there was a problem and it just needed to be fixed, that's all."

Well, one thing's for sure. On that hot afternoon in June in the heart of middle America, my father gave a whole new meaning to the term, "Race to the outhouse."

He not only saved the day for his nephews and great-niece, he taught me a valuable lesson as well.

Quite simply it's this: No matter how grave or impossible a situation seems, just bulldoze ahead. Stop procrastinating. Do something. Go somewhere. Fix it. Don't hesitate. Just do it.

Who knows, you just might end up with a two-foot-tall trophy with a shiny little outhouse on top with the door open, welcoming you inside.

Don't you just love America?

THE END

To order more copies of **Great American Outhouse Stories**, or to inquire about selling this book at a 40% profit for yourself, your church, club, or organization, visit:

www.buybooksontheweb.com

or phone: 1-877-BUY-BOOK
1-877-289-2665

Infinity Publishing will give you a 40% discount on all orders of 5 or more. Orders of 20 or more, Infinity will pay all shipping and handling costs.

Visit author Patricia Lorenz's Web site at:
www.patricialorenz.com